Michael Tomkinson's

GAMBIA

First published 1987 by
Michael Tomkinson Publishing,
Hammamet, Tunisia & POB 429,
London SW1

© Michael Tomkinson 1987

Designed by Roger Davies

Photograph page 84 by Tony Baker/
Picturepoint; pages 9, 11, 22, 23, 27,
28, 29, 30, 31, 32, 80, 82, 85 by Eddie
Brewer OBE; pages 12, 26, 29, 30, 31,
80, 82 by Freddy Graupe; pages 11, 17,
52, 55, 70 by Ann Hills; pages 50, 68,
69, 78, 95 by Michael Kirtley; page 43
by Giorgio Ricatto/Picturepoint; pages
21, 36, 44, 58, 61, 64 by Thomson
Holidays

Printed by South China Printing Co.
in Hong Kong

ISBN 0 905500 19 9

Contents

Introduction

The Gambia is Africa's smallest independent nation, the closest of the English-speaking Commonwealth countries, Britain's first and last West African colony and the tropical resort within easiest reach where winter sun and warmth are guaranteed. The island-capital borders the estuary of the magnificent watercourse from which the modern state derives its name, shape and *raison d'être*. Early adventurers sailed up this 'Golden River' in search of its legendary mines; later traders came, lured by gold and ivory, but soon turning their attention more to lading slaves. For Mungo Park and his lesser-known contemporaries it was the long-sought route to the riches of Timbuktu, to the source of the Niger and even the Nile. While 19th-century officials on the spot palavered, pacified and hunted, their governments, scrambling for Africa, haggled and aggrandized, encompassing the Gambia in artificial frontiers. Today one can travel this rich and vital river, viewing villages and wildlife in places little changed, from the comfort of a pleasure boat, yacht or converted pirogue.

In sunshine rarely interrupted between October and May, in a welcome winter average of 24°, the modern hotels stand for the most part in gardens ablaze with flowers: hibiscus, frangipani, bougainvillea and Morning glory, Golden shower, lantana, jacaranda and canna lilies come as a dazzling contrast to British winter-grey. As colourful and varied as the Gambians' dress, birds abound everywhere, in a brilliant profusion that has made the country famous.

'Gambi-boats' (and wrecks)
by Lasso Wharf, Banjul

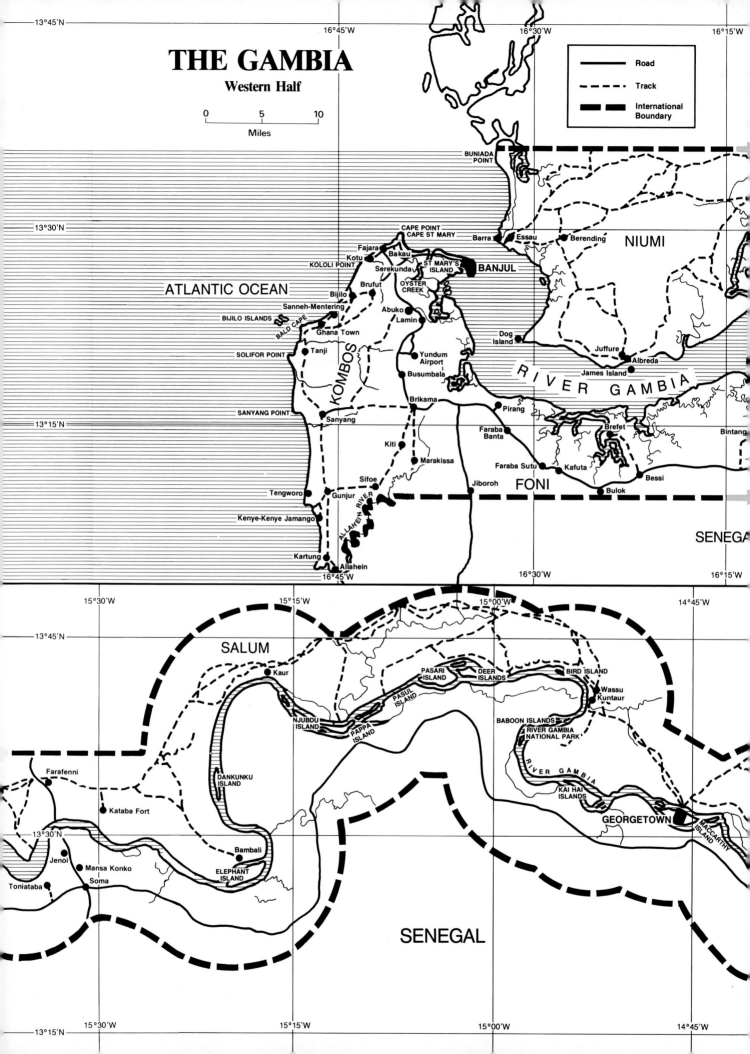

THE GAMBIA
Western Half

0   5   10
Miles

	Road
	Track
	International Boundary

13°45'N   16°45'W   16°30'W   16°15'W

BUNIADA POINT

13°30'N

CAPE POINT
CAPE ST MARY

Barra   Essau   Berending   NIUMI

Fajara   Bakau
Kotu   Serekunda   ST MARY'S ISLAND   BANJUL
KOLOLI POINT

ATLANTIC OCEAN

Bijilo   Brufut
Sanneh-Mentering   OYSTER CREEK
BIJILO ISLANDS   Abuko
BALD CAPE   Lamin
Ghana Town   Dog Island   Juffure

Tanji   Yundum Airport   Albreda
SOLIFOR POINT   James Island

KOMBOS   Busumbala   R I V E R   G A M B I A

13°15'N   Brikama
SANYANG POINT   Pirang

Sanyang   Faraba Banta   Brefet   Bintang

Kiti   Faraba Sutu   Kafuta   Bessi

Marakissa   Jiboroh   Bulok   FONI

Sifoe   SENEGA

Tengworo   Gunjur   ALLAHEIN RIVER

Kenye-Kenye Jamango

Kartung   Allahein
16°45'W

15°30'W   15°15'W   15°00'W   14°45'W

13°45'N

SALUM

Kaur   PASARI ISLAND   DEER ISLANDS   BIRD ISLAND   Wassu
Kuntaur
PASUL ISLAND
NJUBDU ISLAND   BABOON ISLANDS
PAPPA ISLAND   RIVER GAMBIA NATIONAL PARK

Farafenni   R I V E R   G A M B I A

DANKUNKU ISLAND   KAI HAI ISLANDS

Kataba Fort   GEORGETOWN

13°30'N   Bambali   MACCARTHY ISLAND

Jenoi   ELEPHANT ISLAND
Mansa Konko
Toniataba   Soma

SENEGAL

13°15'N   15°30'W   15°15'W   15°00'W   14°45'W

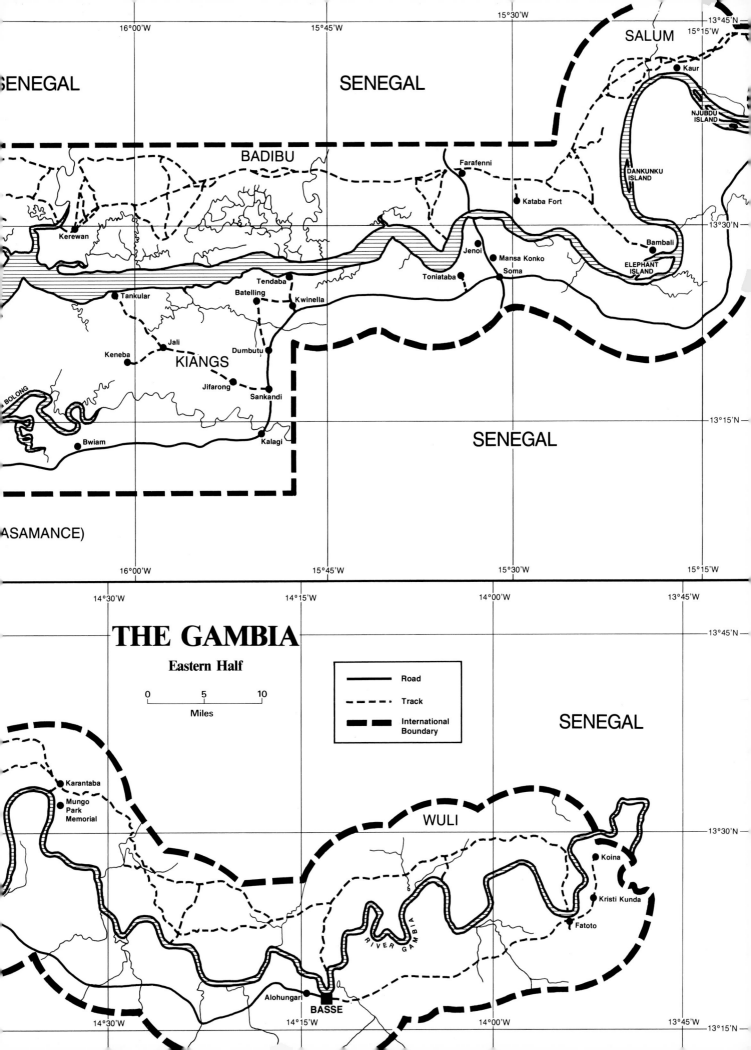

SENEGAL

15°15'W
13°45'N

SALUM

Kaur

NJUBDU
ISLAND

SENEGAL

DANKUNKU
ISLAND

BADIBU

Farafenni

Kataba Fort

13°30'N

Kerewan

Jenoi

Bambali

Mansa Konko

ELEPHANT
ISLAND

Toniataba

Soma

Tendaba

Tankular

Batelling

Kwinella

KIANGS

Jali

Dumbutu

SENEGAL

Keneba

Jifarong

Sankandi

13°15'N

BOLONG

Bwiam

Kalagi

(ASAMANCE)

16°00'W

15°45'W

15°30'W

15°15'W

14°30'W

14°15'W

14°00'W

13°45'W

13°45'N

THE GAMBIA

Eastern Half

0   5   10
Miles

————— Road

- - - - Track

━━ ━━ International
Boundary

SENEGAL

Karantaba

Mungo
Park
Memorial

WULI

13°30'N

Koina

Kristi Kunda

Fatoto

RIVER GAMBIA

Alohungari

BASSE

14°30'W

14°15'W

14°00'W

13°45'W

13°15'N

Outside the hotels, standards should not be overstated: the capital, Banjul, is the largest town – with 60,000 inhabitants; just two arterial roads criss-cross the country; there are roughly a dozen accessible ancient sites, a half-dozen interesting churches and mosques, one nature reserve, one out-of-bounds national park and only three townships with fridges and cold drinks in The Gambia's whole northern half.

But neither should the attractions be under-estimated. The broad sandy beaches, strewn with shells, are everywhere uncrowded. Cottonsilk and baobab trees tower over inland villages where fishermen and farmers gather at the *bantaba*; women pound coos or draw water, their babies on their backs, while dewlapped cattle graze by mountains of groundnuts and high-piled kapok or cotton. Baboons patrol and palm-trees picket the half-farmed savanna all around, which gives way to lush 'jungle' beside the streams and hollows. And through all this courses one of Africa's great waterways, tapering eastward for some 300 miles.

Even more than the bird life and flora, I find the population fascinating. Though small and endowed with few natural resources, The Gambia is by no means a state on sufferance, a post-colonial anachronism. It has a character and identity of its own. Small places, like short men, tend more than others to make an issue of their size: here peoples have moved and married so freely, so blithely – and rightly – ignoring national frontiers, that the country's smallness is compensated by its 'quintessential' richness, by the insight it offers into the region around. One can holiday in Kenya and learn nothing of its neighbours, visit Tunisia without suffering the side-effects of Libya and Algeria, but The Gambia means an encounter with West Africa.

Canna lilies *passim*

Gunjur beach at daybreak

Landing edible *cymbium glans* molluscs, Ghana Town

6

Geography. The Gambia is the westernmost country of Africa and lies astride longitude 15° west. It is equidistant from the Equator and Tropic of Cancer, 13°15-13°30 being the approximate latitudinal extent. In common with many of its African neighbours, the country is the victim of some geodetic dithering: elastic dimensions and an area that varies with each official source. The *Commonwealth Fact Sheet* of 1977 gives a total of 4049 square miles (10,367 square kilometres), the government's *The Gambia in Brief* 4045 square miles (10,356 km^2). With its 4003 square miles (10,247 km^2) the *Encyclopaedia Britannica* further reduces the country's size. Whatever the actual extent, it is easily half as large again as Lincolnshire.

The northern and southern boundaries, both with Senegal, are at their widest 30 miles (48 kms) apart. From this distance on the coast they narrow inland to sixteen miles (24 kms) – the maximum range, according to Whitehall wags, of British gunboats on the river. State and river stretch eastward for 304 miles/487 kms (or 201 miles/322 kms or 288 miles/460 kms viz. the above authorities) as far as the Barrakunda Falls, whereas landfall in the other direction is in the West Indies, 3000 miles away. The last remark is not fatuous: it helps explain The Gambia's involvement with the slave-trade. Wind and water aided and abetted: the Canary current carried ships south to the mouth of the river. While the doldrums then impeded their further passage round Africa, the north equatorial current and the prevailing north-east trade winds (not named that for nothing) combined to assist them across the Atlantic.

Venturing southward beyond Cape Non ('No further'), early European navigators faced the flat inhospitable coast of the Spanish Sahara and Mauritania, 1100 miles with little water and few natural harbours, until the

The River Gambia, 'ferry' at Fatoto

8

Purple heron

Lagoon, Kartung

The ferry crossing, Kerewan

9

Dawn chores near Tendaba

Lilytrotter 'grooming'

Senegal, Gambia and Casamance rivers were reached. All three rise in the Guinea plateau of Futa Jallon, the Gambia twelve miles from the 'town' of Labe. From here the distance to the sea is as the crow flies 150 miles, to the actual estuary about 300, but the river's meanderings protract its total length to over 1000 miles. Its initial width of 600 feet is constricted to a twenty-foot channel by the Barrakunda Falls. For most writers these ledges of laterite rock are an 'obstacle to navigation': the present-day scarcity of boats above Fatoto makes the comment academic. For The Gambia the falls' significance is as the country's easternmost limit, below which the river is tidal. Koina is the first 'port' (viz. rickety jetty), Kristi Kunda ('Christ's Place') the first, now-defunct Anglican mission; at Fatoto is the first (small-dinghy) ferry.

Here the picturesque river-banks impress with an average height of 40 feet, which varies with the rainfall and the tide. They illustrate how for the last million years the river has gouged its course through the tertiary sandstone of the Senegambian plateau. Islands of harder ironstone and gneiss have resisted its erosion and now stand as isolated, flat-topped hills; pockets of kaolin supply the cottage-potteries near Basse. From here to the Atlantic, on terra firma everywhere, the topsoil is in general red laterite, an infertile 'ferruginous crust' that frustrates farmers but, like East Africa's murram, makes good 'roads'. It covers all too much of the country and, on any dry-season drive, the wayside vegetation, your vehicle and you.

A Barrakunda-like formation, the Buruko Rocks, again constricts the river. Squeezed into a channel only 100 feet wide, the faster current sweeps with it a mass of silt and sand; the alluvium removed in the upper reaches reforms as islands in the rambling middle river. Below MacCarthy Island, or Janjangbure, they are named either from their part-extinct fauna – Baboon, Bird, Deer and Elephant – or, with many an alias, in the vernacular: Kai Hai, Pasari, Pasul and Pappa, Njubdu and Dankunku. Human habitation consists of Georgetown on MacCarthy Island and, on the Baboon Islands, the National Park wardens in remote confinement and the occasional Western visitor to a study-group of chimpanzees.

The *Jamond* off Lamin

The river's meanderings round these sometimes waterlogged obstacles meant 80 miles of difficult tacking in the days of sail: only with the advent of steam could Georgetown be easily reached and developed. Kuntaur is the all-time limit for ocean-going vessels and marks the approximate point at which salinity yields to fresh water. (Salt water, to be precise, reaches in the dry season 140 miles up stream, and half that far during the rains.)

In riverside clearings decrepit piers step from the water to narrow mud causeways that run straight to villages built high and dry behind. They stand on slight rises, amidst the banto faros. Meaning in Mandinka 'beyond the swamp', these grasslands, often flooded by river and rain, are for the rest cultivable, if salinity permits. In its final 93 miles below Elephant Island the broader straighter river sidles off into larger creeks, here called bolons/bolongs. Many, like the largest Bintang Bolong, straggle north or south into Senegal; tortuous tributaries, they none the less contribute a dribble of fresh water when replenished by rain. Their banks, like those of the mainstream, are a tangle of mangrove swamps: not the Indian Ocean's lowly growth but off-shore forests in which air-roots arc symmetrically high and timber-straight trunks stand 60 feet tall.

As fertility deteriorates towards the river mouth – clay alluvium and sand predominating – the Gambia grows busier and more magnificent. Fishermen cast hand-nets from mahogany dug-outs and painted-plank canoes; tugs chug down with lighters of groundnuts in tow; birds, as everywhere, astonish at every turn and dolphins frolic or bask like shark as you sail by.

En route you pass, as did the earliest settlers, two islands of not alluvium but rock. If the river is the axis round which the country's life turns, James Island was for centuries the hub. Dog Island – down stream, accessible by foot at low tide – was first manned by Britain in 1661. St Andrew's/James Island – in mid-river, more extensive and defensible – had been frequented by the Portuguese since 1456. And sailing in untroubled by sand-banks or reefs (the estuary's 'bar' is navigable and in the river's silt no coral grows) Hollanders, Frenchmen and the Duke of Courland's Germans had fought with them and died for these petty arid outcrops.

On the last and largest island stands the capital, Banjul. Despite a swampy, once-waterlogged site which, in Sir Richard Burton's words, was 'selected for proximity to mud, mangoes, malaria and miasma', Britain in 1816 established colonial Bathurst. From twelve miles at its widest, between Cape St Mary and Buniada Point, the Gambia estuary narrows here to under three. Thus initially of strategic importance, the new capital acquired both commercial and administrative significance as the British colony/protectorate took shape. Finally demarcated in 1889, that shape prompted the Victorian comment that 'its very appearance on the map is an invitation to the zealous reformer'. American journalists prefer the analogy of 'a long crooked finger poked into Senegal'.

Climate. Where the weather is concerned, this is Europe's antipodes, and Britain's better half. In September or October the rains ease off and there starts a sunny season that lasts until April or May. The north-east trade winds keep temperatures on the coast at an equable and pleasant average of 24°/76° Fahrenheit. During the seven-month tourist season the thermometer drops to December, with the last 30 years' median *minimum* of 16°/61°F. From January to May it climbs back to the October-November 'peak', measured over the same period as a *maximum* 32°/91°F. At this

Immature lilytrotter

Flooded banto faros, near Farafenni

Air-roots of the mangroves, along any bolong

The Gambia is lacking in mineral resources. The gold-mines for which it enjoyed chimeric fame have proved as elusive as the Philosopher's stone; ilmenite workings have been abandoned; the 'immense deposits of iron ore on the cliffs overhanging the river' are exploited only by armchair geographers, and salt – dried from the shallows and bolongs and packed in roadside baskets for transportation to market – is the only claim to geological wealth.

Middle-river settlement, beneath the ubiquitous oil-palms and kapok trees

time of year humidity, too, is at an ideal average of 50-60%. Days are warm and nights cool.

Climatically The Gambia teeters on the edge of the arid Sahel zone. The coast generally benefits from the ocean's tempering effect, but inland the Atlantic's sphere of influence is soon replaced by the Sahel's. The heat increases as humidity, and even visibility, drop. Especially when the north wind blows – the hazy *harmattan*, between February and May, for a week or two at a time – throats parch, lips crack and 'static' is crisp in the atmosphere. At such times the baobab tree prevents loss of water by shedding its leaves: man's only recourse is drink.

A word about the wet season may be of deterrent interest. As every schoolboy knows, the air in the Sahara rises with the heat of summer, causing an area of low pressure which induces the south-west monsoons. Blowing from the ocean, these arrive laden with rain. In their first encounter with the weakening north-east trades (what scientists call the Inter-tropical Front) they deposit it on The Gambia in spectacular storms and tornados. (Wind and water have similar confrontations: when the cool Canary current meets the warmer Guinea stream, fogs occur on the Senegambian coast.) As the monsoons set in, ousting the trade winds between May and July, the air is hot and heavy, the rainfall welcome but variable in force. While showers leave, momentarily, clear skies and cooler air, cloudbursts bring inches in minutes.

Though the sand and permeable soils drain too fast for streams and pools to survive for long, the vegetation then is at its most luxuriant. The climax is August, when humidity of 100% can make the mornings misty. From 4° at daybreak, the temperature has been known to attain 38° by midday.

To see the Gambian dawn and sunrise does not mean, as so often, losing sleep. The day breaks at a civilized 7 a.m., give or take twenty minutes either way. Nightfall gives itself similar leeway: if lighting-up time existed here it would be around 7-7.30 p.m.

Agriculture. The rainfall during the monsoon season is a *sine qua non* for The Gambia's farmers, whose bane is its unpredictable start and finish, and on occasions its failure to appear. Farming is none the less the nation's mainstay, accounting for 94% of its foreign exchange, 60% of per capita income and, with fishing, 85% of the work-force.

Besides giving front-page prominence to the groundnut 'results', the official *Gambia News Bulletin* exhorts its readers to 'Light up with Briquettes'. This solid fuel, from compacted groundnut-shells, is sold cheaply in lieu of the charcoal with which too many village housewives cook and heat. Its manufacturers, however, cut and burn whole forests, destroying the habitat of many wildlife species and also the vegetation cover. This causes steady 'desertification' and The Gambia, like many African states, has banned random charcoal-burning.

The need to conserve the oil-palm explains the prohibition of another once-popular product: palm-toddy. Bainunka men, especially in the Kombos, you could see scale the footholed trunk with their fixed elliptical sling – like nothing so much as a windsurfing boom. They tapped the tree just below the flower-stalk and, lax Muslims, then sold off what little they left unconsumed of the fast-fermenting liquor. (A dance done by the Gambia National Troupe depicts *Cassa*-tappers in their *daaka,* palm-wine 'brewery'.) Nowadays only small-time tapping is allowed, just enough to jollify friends and family. For removal of the sap not only impairs the oil, it has also made of the palm itself an endangered species. Some fruit is boiled

The Senegambia craft market, making local cotton cloth

Pounding *coos*

and crushed, the palm-oil one tastes in local dishes exuding from the flesh, the mesocarp. But the oil from the kernels being worth more, these are more often bagged and exported – by the GPMB to the EEC.

Longer heads have always thought that The Gambia's reliance on the 'cash monoculture' of groundnuts was unwise. The alternative, or rather adjunct, of cotton has often been mooted – especially in the 19th century when Americans were prospering on southern plantations and Britain's Victorians, rich from India, were turning Egypt from self-sufficiency in wheat to dependence on international cotton-price fluctuations. Here the crop has a long and chequered history. Reaching the Gambia in 1455, the Portuguese explorer Luiz de Cadamosto was 'astonished to find the inhabitants clothed'. For centuries the Serahulis, Fulas and Mandinkas had grown 'tree cotton' from which to make the *pagnes* they dyed with indigo. In 1760, impressed by Senegambian samples, the London Society of Arts had offered a gold medal for the importer of the greatest quantity, 'not less than two tons', but only in 1833 was that amount first attained. Settling the Liberated Africans up river, the 'Home Government' supplied them with Sea Island cotton-seed, from which 26 tons were shipped in 1838. An official report of 1860 gave 206 tons as grown and traded annually: 'If cultivation . . . is now taken up seriously,' it said, 'the export return should shortly become substantial'. 'Shortly' was not until 1904, when 70 tons left Bathurst for London. There the British Cotton Growing Association had been set up in 1902; in 1903 £500,000 were found for advances to planters and experimental farms, for seed, ginneries and baling machines; King Edward in 1904 gave his blessing by way of a Royal Charter . . . and in 1906 all Bathurst could report was that 'cotton might be taken up . . . if it is seen to pay'. *Plus ça change*, it seems. In 1965 the Agriculture Department launched a new Cotton Programme; a pilot project for commercial production followed in 1969; 1976 saw a ginnery built at Basse, but despite sales of 2405 tons in 1983, the GPMB regretted that 'the target production level has still not been achieved'.

Groundnuts are the corner-stone of agriculture, the economy and, in a sense, The Gambia itself. Known as *tio* to the locals, the 'peanut' or 'monkey nut' is the country's only significant export and principal cash crop, Senegal and The Gambia being the world's largest commercial producers. So vital are the unsightly swellings on the roots of this legume that books like Lady Southorn's *The Gambia* are sub-titled *The Story of the Groundnut Colony*. And when that colony became independent the plant was chosen to top its coat of arms, which featured *dibongo*s and *dabandingo*s, the coop coops or hoes used to till it.

The Portuguese in the 16th century introduced the species from Brazil; the Gambians until the 1830s cultivated it for their own consumption only. Several odd quirks of colonial history were to be the cause and effect of its rapid development. Soap came into fashion in France (more so, it seems, than in Britain) and demand for groundnuts as its raw material grew: from 100 baskets in 1830 to a record 8636 tons in 1848. Soon overtaking hides, ivory and bees-wax, the crop constituted by the 1850s over two thirds of the colony's export total. Production increased with Britain's colonial commitment. Agricultural advisers brought in new strains like the 'Rio Fresco'/Rufisque, spread the use of fertilizers and implemented oxen-ization, prevailing upon villagers to use animals in lieu of the coop coop. By resisting the enticement to mechanize – tractors break down – The Gambia was able to progress simply while other African projects like Tanganyika's Groundnut Scheme turned into costly fiascos. Recovering from the natural set-backs of drought in the early 1960s, an overdose of rain in 1978 and drought again in 1982-83, output now stands at an annual average of 80,000 tons, which may mean £30 million in revenue or, as in 1982-83, a 'large trading loss'.

For five pence (50 bututs) the women on sidewalks and in market-places everywhere will measure you out, from their cheap Chinese bowls, a tomato puree tinful of crisp fresh-roasted nuts. Such 'Hand Picked Selected' and 'Philippine Pinks' may still be grown 'exclusively for the confectionery trade' but peanuts, neat, have long been of less import-ance than the oil pressed from them. The basis for French soap, and the crop's initial success, this 'side-product' soon so dominated the market that already in the 1860s Gambian nuts were hit by competition from American petroleum and 'belmontine'. The Tanganyikan scheme had been designed to relieve the world's post-War shortage of margarine; edible oil from groundnut kernels, refined without odour or taste, fights a losing battle with olive-oil in the tariff-bound markets of the EEC. The Gambia's two oil-mills now process 40% of the crop and, together with 'expeller cake' as animal feed, derivatives are still being studied. Partly to reduce our dependence on petroleum, partly to avert a pro-duce 'mountain' (caused by the Senegambia, USA and India), American scientists are looking to the groundnut as a source of new foodstuffs and ersatz petrol, paper, cosmetics and industrial diamonds.

The farmers up river would be flattered if they knew. Each season they clear the bush where necessary in the time-honoured African way, by the ubiquitous 'slash and burn' technique. Joined seasonally by 'strange farmers' – 5-10,000 share-cropping *nawettanes* from Mali, Guinea, Sudan and Senegal – they brush the fields ready for the first soil-softening rain. They sometimes fertilize, then they (or more often now their oxen) plough. Planting takes place at the start of the monsoon; weeding is easy (which is why this is all-male work); picking begins as the wet season ends (given the requisite 750 mm of rain and a minimum temperature of 24°). After two or three seasons of this, and a one-year sortie into cereals, natural nutrients in the sandy soil are exhausted and the land, if not

Winnowing freshly picked groundnuts, Tendaba

Loading a groundnut lighter, Basse

fertilized, should be left to lie fallow and revert to bush.

The plants are laid to dry on platforms, raised and covered to safeguard them respectively from vermin and belated rain. The villagers next beat the nuts free with forked sticks; they 'winnow' them either in the women's loose-meshed panniers or in the rotating *passoires*, the long perforated cylinders one sees in many villages. Collected and piled in open-air *seccos* or the larger centres' hangar-like 'bins', then graded, weighed and transported by lorry or lighter, 'quality' nuts – from December to March – go for decortication at Kaur or Banjul; to these towns' wharves for direct shipment overseas or, for crushing into oil and 'cake', to Banjul's Denton Bridge. If 'Sub-standard' or 'Black and Mouldy', they end up as 'sludge' for the soap factory next door.

All this, like palm-kernels, rice and cotton, is controlled since 1973 by the Gambia Produce Marketing Board. For generations groundnut-growers here had been an unwitting object-lesson for Rabelais' *Discourses in the Praise of Borrowers and Lenders*. The need to feed families through each year's rainy season, to buy seed for sowing and wait months for any return had made them dependent on advances of food and/or funds. Crop failure put them irretrievably in debt: to the pioneer French firms like the CFAO, Maurel Frères and (until 1978) Maurel & Prom, to Lebanese traders and less scrupulous 'julamen' lending at 100% plus. To keep hungry growers from eating the seed-nuts, and reducing the crop by picking prematurely for the sake of an early return, the colonial government in 1903 stepped in to subsidize, store and distribute. Which resulted simply in a transfer of the farmers' debt from the dealers to HMG. Owed £50,000 by 1921, Britain altered course. In 1924 an Agriculture Department was started, later a programme of expatriate advisers and local 'extension workers' to organize seed-storage on a village basis, to encourage mixed farming and – the most far-reaching move – to innovate co-operatives. Nowadays the Gambia Co-operative Union accounts for 60% of sales from growers to the GPMB; one surviving Lebanese firm and around 30 Gambians are the private 'Licensed Buying Agents' that handle the balance. The Gambia Commercial & Development Bank makes the still-needed advances; the Gambia River Transport Company's seven barges provide lighterage at fixed 'zonal freight rates' and, building to date ten produce depots, setting up annually about 100 buying stations, subsidizing fertilizers and holding 'price stabilization reserves', the GPMB has succeeded over the last ten years in increasing threefold the prices paid to growers.

The River Gambia, a 'Gambi-boat' in full sail

Raising livestock alongside crops was an obvious corollary to the government's encouragement of home meat-production (and of the use of fertilizers, since cattle in particular guarantee an instant, on-the-spot supply). Ninety per cent of the livestock here are cattle – humped zebus or smaller tsetse-resistant *ndamas* cross-bred from the zebu and the West African Dwarf. The Fulas are the country's cowboys, sometimes owning a few head themselves, more often tending the collective herds of others. They traditionally see their scrawny kine as a token of wealth, not a source of food. Though it could often improve the stock, they (like Kenya's Masai) would no more cull their herds than you would take three clean pounds for a dirty fiver. To combat this reluctance to slaughter, the government banned meat imports in 1968.

Replacing the endemic 'tree' with hardier 'hairy' cotton, planters moved to Nigerian varieties then settled on 'American Upland'. Ploughing and harrowing for sowing must be deep. Sowing must be done by hand, in precisely the right week or two, with the soil just sufficiently moist. No moisture must touch the bolls during picking . . . Growing only on the well-drained sandy soils of the middle and upper river, where groundnuts also fare best (and require much less effort of the selfsame work-force), cotton looks likely to remain for some time a perennially 'promising' crop.

Rubber and gum are bygones. Exports of the former stopped in 1901, 'no doubt because . . . the trees, not being judiciously tapped, withered and died'. The 'rubber-trees' seen nowadays are ornamental relics. Humble gum (*gomme arabique*) became a Franco-British *casus belli* in the 18th and 19th centuries, when each country's African Company took up arms over the bacterial pus of the *Acacia senegalensis*. In moments of truce they traded the commodity for slaves: 360,000 pounds of the one for 100 of the other 'in their prime'. So important was the gum of Portendic that, although in 1783 all Senegal was surrendered, British rights to the trade were conceded by the French (who demanded and obtained in return the enclave of Albreda). Contending nevertheless with French seizure of their ships and sabotage of supplies, Bathurst's merchants maintained the commerce until in 1857 Albreda and the rights at Portendic were re-exchanged.

Rice is a staple of long standing. As its cultivation needs more care, men entrust it to the women. Traditionally they have utilized the upland areas where the banto faros are no longer too salt and the river-banks not yet too high for flooding. Though covering only one tenth of the area under such 'rainfed' cultivation, irrigated paddies are the hope for the future. The men accept to help build the bunds, the banks of mud bound with grass around each paddy. The women plough, sometimes plant stake-fences to deter hungry hippos, transplant from the nurseries the six-inch seedlings, and weed – at the same time of year as their men tend the groundnuts. In December, with the waters subsided, the ripe stalks are cut one by one. Each day's harvest is then threshed: on the ground, thrashed with sticks in the villages, churned in some centres' hand-operated drums or milled, in privileged places like Basse, by machine.

These techniques are basically Indian, but present-day Chinese were an obvious choice for advice. One of The Gambia's few memorials, on the south bank by MacCarthy Island, honours the Mr Lee who led the first team of Taiwanese in 1966-69. In 1973 the government's Development Project was started, and in 1984 the first harvest reaped at Jahali Pachaar. A show-piece of successful irrigation, the 3700 acres around these two centres promptly repaid a £23-million investment with a twice-yearly crop averaging seventeen tonnes per acre. This, to the amazement not only of its Euroconsult supervisers, is a rice output unparalleled anywhere in the world.

Growing thickly on tall trees around Banjul, The Gambia's grapefruit and Java oranges are in the spring a surprising sight. They are also for the most part pip (which is why the latter are usually peeled, sold off-white in the thick pith and just sucked). Limes are more amenable: a 100-acre estate at Yundum supplies since 1967 a factory producing 'single strength juice' and, from the peel, exported lime-oil.

Sheep and goats straggle everywhere, especially over your road by night. Their skins and hides, no longer wild animals', are a minor item on the country's list of exports. Odd domestic pigs are an unexpected sight near Serekunda: salvaging on sufferance amongst Muslim compounds,

Citrus stall, with bananas, pineapples and packed groundnuts

Papayas ready for picking

they are butchered and sold in Banjul's Albert Market. Chickens were the victim of a Gambian fiasco to match Tanganyika's Groundnut Scheme. In 1948 Britain's Colonial Development Corporation allotted funds for a 'Mass Production Poultry Scheme' at Yundum. An American director was appointed, but his knowledge of local conditions was nil. Fowl typhoid in 1950 killed 80,000 chickens, the project depended on local feedstuffs which it proved impossible to find, Gambians objected that their short supplies of food were made even scarcer by the scheme and in 1951 it was abandoned. Losses were £628,000: the 38,520 eggs produced had cost the British tax-payer £20·77 apiece. The late Yundum College was installed in the premises. The government has ever since left poultry to the private sector.

Vegetation. To the north of The Gambia, Sudan savanna deteriorates into desert; to the south, gallery and tropical rain forest engulfs equatorial Africa. The *cordon sanitaire* of these botanical extremes is formed by their lesser-scale counterparts: the South Guinea savanna and the South Guinea woodland. Ecologically The Gambia extends into both, and its flora in particular is correspondingly rich.

The hibiscus, dying daily, adorns the paths at Kotu Strand and at Bakotu; the Tropic Gardens boasts several more varieties, and many of them double: yellow, orange, red, pink and white, 'Sleeping', Korean and the Japanese *Grandiflora*.

Bougainvillea, in the tropics and the Mediterranean area, is an unpredictable boon. In East Africa it spreads, entwined on wire frames, as a multicoloured carpet – mauve, magenta, mustard, salmon or white – but often declines to climb up or cascade down walls. Which is the only way it will grow around the Mediterranean, stockily covering vertical surfaces but refusing to grow low along the ground. In The Gambia it not only creeps and leans but also, as bushes, forms lengthy hedges: like English privet at Bungalow Beach or, at the Fajara, solid circles of colour. At Kotu Strand Village the tamarisk, too, is clipped and trimmed into hedges.

Hedge of bougainvillea, Kotu beach

Walls and corrugated-iron roofs are camouflaged convolvulus-mauve, with not convolvulus but *Thunbergia grandiflora.* The orchid-like Dutchman's Pipe climbs; Golden shower descends like orange honeysuckle. Convolvulus and honeysuckle, poinsettias, jasmin and sturdy oleander, night-fragrant *Datura* ('Angel's trumpet') and *Lagastroemia* ('Queen of the Flowers') all flourish beside the jacaranda and banana-plant, its flowers weird-obscene, the long-podded flame-tree and oddities like the Century palm, which lives for 100 years, flowers once and dies.

Golden shower

African crocus

Ground orchid

Thunbergia grandiflora

23

Natural forests are suffering, as everywhere, from the 20th century. One third of The Gambia's has vanished since independence, burned, cut or cleared for charcoal, timber or farms. But impressive patches survive: in forest parks which cover three per cent of the country and, easily accessible, at Abuko. Here the lowlier savanna growth yields to closer riverine 'jungle'. The Grey plum's buttress-roots block the way like fallen trunks; aerial and stilt-roots from the parasitic figs rise, entwined with dangling lianas; tallos and Elephant trees ('African breadfruit') stand massive; with incredible foliage, the Cabbage or Candelabra trees add to the natural chiarascuro.

Abuko

The raffia-palm provides fibre for fencing, matting and furniture, sap for palm-toddy and polished seeds as beads for bracelets and ornamental knick-knacks. The rhun or fan-palm is easily recognized by the leaf-form from which it takes its name and the standard borassus-bulge in its 100-foot trunk. Insect repelling and not rotting in salt water, this goes into bridges, wharves and roofing, while lower leaves serve as fencing or poles. The Swamp date-palm prefers freshwater swamps, where it forms impenetrable clumps. Like the straggling rattan it is technically a vine.

A rural compound anywhere, typically fenced with bamboo *krinting*

The bamboo's 1000 species are the fastest growing of all living things, and 1000 known applications make it the world's most versatile. Here it helps bind the soil against erosion, and was widely burned until the recent ban – for charcoal, no longer as a cure for prickly heat. From the bamboo's stalk comes The Gambia's *krinting* which for walls and fencing vies with corrugated iron; its shoots have not yet reached Fajara's Bamboo Restaurant, and it bursts into blossom only once, before dying, each decade or two.

The savanna, more widespread than woodland, is also less dramatic: low loose-knit bush over which lone trees tower, grass-green in our autumn, parched brown by Christmas and often burned black in the spring. Scattered amidst the tracts scarred by shifting cultivation stand trees such as the Custard apple and the West African Gum copal; the African locust bean, the emetic Guinea peach and the much sought-after kola; the Black and the Gingerbread plum; ironwood, rosewood and Velvet tamarind; acacias like the fire-resistant winterthorn which, a perverse exception, sheds its leaves in the rainy season; cassias like the West African laburnum, with seed-pods poisonous and its roots an aphrodisiac.

The cottonsilk/kapok tree dominates the savanna, in both abundance and size. The Gambia's 'White-flowered silk cotton' is larger and more striking than its namesake in East Africa. Like the mango there, it often guards the village 'square': by the *bentengo* (platform) in the shade of this *bantango* is the *bantaba* (meeting-place). Buttressed by astonishing 'natural planks', its six-foot-wide trunk rises over 100 feet, providing a mass of albeit inferior timber for dug-outs, drums and not very durable coffins. From the seed-pods bursts the white floss (kapok) which fills mattresses, pillows and unreliable lifebelts.

The baobab, that tropical oddity, stands as the sentinel (or marks the long-gone spot) of every settlement. With boughs like roots, it is obviously growing upside down . . . doomed to do so, Africans say, because it would not stay where God placed it. They nevertheless make cold drinks and lollipops from the crisp white contents of its pods; grind flour from its 'monkey-bread' fruit, boil and eat its young leaves and strip it symmetrically, like cork-oaks in the Atlas, of the bark which is shredded for fibre.

Baobab trees, James Island

Wildlife. Though the Gambian savanna boasts these tallest African trees, its surviving animals are, apart from hippos, smaller scale. The elephant, as collectors of colonial postage stamps know, was once the national emblem; ivory was traded here in bulk; since 1913 the only memento is the place-name Elephant Island. The last of the once-common Western giraffes was drowned near MacCarthy Island in 1899; in 1911 the last Giant or 'Derbian' eland was killed. The West African and the 'bastard' Korrigum hartebeest, the buffalo, Roan antelope, waterbuck and kob have all shared the same fate. Each year still a lion or two is reported from the region of Kuntaur. But these are 'outstanding faunal events' and what features in the official picture-book as 'the King of the African jungle, and particularly that of the Gambia' is a monarch in exile, caged at Abuko with his unintended offspring, and flown in 'courtesy of British Caledonian.'

With the President's Banjul Declaration, however, a new concern for wildlife became official policy. On 18 February 1977 Sir Dawda Jawara's Independence Day speech pledged his government's 'untiring efforts to conserve for now and posterity as wide a spectrum as possible of our remaining fauna and flora'. Words became deeds with the Wildlife Conservation Act of 1977, which outlawed hunting and the trade in animal products. With the Abuko Nature Reserve established in March 1968, the five Baboon Islands were gazetted in November 1978 as the 1448-acre River Gambia National Park. The *éminence grise* of The Gambia's ecology, the 'saviour' of its wildlife in a sense, is a former forestry officer, E.F. Brewer OBE. Named in 1976 the first Director of Wildlife Conservation, he prompted the country's admirable programme and, through the Wildlife Department, works to maintain its momentum.

The common Vervet monkey, called more correctly *callitrix*, is a member of the Green monkey family. The black face is framed by a spiky white halo of whiskers; the belly is silver, the back olive-green, and the whole thing frequently seen.

Part of Stella Brewer's early life was devoted to rehabilitating chimpanzees. Her protégés – first in Senegal's Niokolo Koba, later in the River Gambia Park – were all first-generation immigrants, either confiscated from traders breaking the law or saved as orphans, circus-surplus or cast-off pets from overseas. The Gambia's last wild chimpanzees survived just into this century, and only in transit through Abuko will you see these tailless apes now: not in the outback or in the national park, where the study-groups are safeguarded with justifiable scientific jealousy. Read Stella Brewer's *Forest Dwellers* instead. The Russians paid more than for *Life on Earth* for the rights to this homely and moving account of her success in training all-too-human chimps to survive in their natural environment. Filmed by Hugo van Lawick in 1976, the book takes her story up to 1977. An American, Janis Carter, subsequently conducted a similar project, living devotedly and usually alone on another of the national park islands. Though one of her retinue 'speaks' sign language, she had also to practise and not preach as the only way of teaching: building and 'sleeping' on leaf nests twenty feet up; emitting 'good food grunts' and 'enjoying' seeds and

fruit; 'fishing' with a stick for ants, to be licked off and swallowed before they sting . . . but saved by the chimpanzees' unsuspected instinct from having to show them how to catch, smash and make a Chinese meal of other monkeys.

Abuko's 100-odd Western red colobus have also been the object of an American girl's PhD research. This took almost four years, and in a quick trip through the forest, savanna or swamp you should hope for no more than a treetop glimpse of these thumbless, black-backed and russet-fronted primates. Of the colobus' sixteen sub-species, the *Badius temminckii* lives only in The Gambia and Senegal, and in troops of 30-40 in which 'female adults are the most socially mobile' and 'males go out of their way to engage females in friendly behaviors'.

Red colobus, mother grooming infant

The Red Patas monkey's ability to run at twenty mph and its 'home range' of twenty square miles are the reasons why it so often frustrates photographers. Researchers into its feeding habits too, since each troop's treetop sentinel prevents any close approach and the animals shot by villagers have all too often a bellyful filched from their fields. Aids to identification are the long legs, bushy eyebrows and dull orange fur.

now said to survive above Elephant Island. Here they surface – piggy ears and monstrous muzzles – to delight passers-by on their boats. And, if approached too close or escorting their young, also charge, ram and try to capsize them. The hippopotamus gives birth on land, suckles underwater and lives some 30 years. Though able to wander ten miles by night, and even outrun a man, it rarely does either as in places the banks at low tide impede it and elsewhere the riverside paddies provide the daily 300-400 pounds it must eat to sustain its two tons.

Crocodiles flourish in three species here: the 'Blunt-nosed' Nile variety, the long-snouted *Cataphractus* (Africa's gharial/gavial) and the Pygmy. The first-named are those that pretend to doze by Abuko's Bambo Pool (*bambo* being Mandinka for crocodile) or splash disappointingly, leaving ripples on the bolong, when they see you too soon in your Tendaba canoe. They also tend to disappoint on the 'crocodile pools'. To Katchikali, Kartung and Berending childless wives and unsuccessful

Red Patas monkeys drinking

The Western baboon (*gong* in Wolof) frequents open country, with a few rocks for preference. A redder version of West Africa's Olive baboon, the Gambian variety feeds mainly on grass, seeds and fruit, though fancies on occasions hares, birds, other monkeys and crops. It seeks safety in numbers, of up to 300 per troop.

Lounging in the track ahead or loping off over the fields, youngsters clinging to mother's under-carriage while the maned and dog-faced patriarchs bark, baboons are for visitors a regular diversion. For farmers a regular pest. Never hunted here for food, they roam fearlessly close to civilization. They steer clear however of leopards, whose natural enemy (and favourite food) they are.

Hippopotamuses were protected during the British protectorate, with a £100 penalty for poaching. But barely 100 are

Nile crocodile

businessmen travel from distant villages to see the venerated reptiles. Visitors blanch as black pilgrims descend in the hope of being blessed with a sight of the Sacred White One. If seeing is believing, I have grounds for doubting the last. The odd smallish specimens that might deign appear will sleep on oblivious, jaws ajar. Or waddle off alarmed if approached by sceptical infidels.

Its ability to generate babies and/or business is debatable, but the crocodile proves its usefulness to fishermen by eating the river's predatory catfish. These it swallows fresh and whole. Small animals are swept from the water's edge by its tail, held under and drowned in its jaws, then hidden on the bank and eaten later, very 'high'. Plovers pick parasites from backs (not *pace* Herodotus, from between teeth), new sets of teeth grow until the age of 80 and the malignly primaeval appearance is not deceptive: little changed since the Mesozoic era, crocodiles are sole survivors of the archosaur family of dinosaurs. Mothers lay and incubate up to 100 eggs, help their squeaking offspring break from the shells, then safeguard them, sometimes, from mongooses and monitors.

The tail of the Gambian mongoose accounts for half of its fourteen inches. It is also long, thick and straight, not squirrel-bushy, on The Gambia's other self-explanatory types: Dwarf, Marsh, Long-nosed and White-tailed. Mongooses endear themselves to man, or to readers of the *Jungle Book* at least, by engaging snakes in lone combat. But only if given no choice. Normally they prefer to hunt in packs: for mice, birds and lizards by day in the savanna, or for chickens from compounds by night. Its numbers help distinguish the species from squirrels which, as in Europe, are seen at most in pairs.

Duikers are the charmingly diminutive, dainty-footed antelopes of which the Maxwell's sub-species can be seen, almost tame, at Abuko. The Western Harnessed antelopes there too are 'inscribed' with white lines on flanks and shoulders and patterned white dots on the rump. Formerly more abundant and trusting, they could in the 1900s 'be seen running fearlessly about the streets of Bathurst . . . a common feature in the grounds of Government House'. An aquatic contrast, the sitatunga, is said to survive in 'middle river'. Its feet that splay in water like a camel's in sand give

Grimm's duiker, juvenile

West African sitatunga, male and female

it exclusive right of entry to inaccessible swamps, and make it a 'difficult animal to meet with'. Observed more easily at Abuko, the *Tragelaphus Spekei* takes its name from the Victorian explorer who, besides discovering the source of the Nile, first found it knee-deep in East Africa. Bohor reedbuck are still reported from the north bank, oribi in the east, but neither in any number.

Hyaenas are now known to kill for themselves and not merely scavenge. They do both neatly and hygienically, devouring even carcasses and so clearing the savanna of every last bone. In a consequently well-scoured enclosure at Abuko the seventeen born here of 'Buki and Buster', the first 'imported' pair, have an air of cuddly though cringing domesticity. In 1902 the colonial Governor sent the London Zoo a Gambian hyaena which soon became the 'best behaved and tamest in the Gardens'.

The warthog (by the zoologists' curious expedient of counting toes) is related to the hippopotamus. It grubs up roots and crops (the 'warts' protecting the face?) and, when alarmed, trots podgily off, tail erect and family following in order of importance. The warthog is here called 'bush pig' so that visitors can confuse it with the African bush pig *alias* Red hog or Red river hog. No confusion occurs to local minds: the latter is too rare.

Rarely seen creatures are responsible for the most frequent natural feature of the Gambian savanna: blind, soft-bodied termites that bind the earth with half-digested cellulose to build the astonishing peaks, pinnacles, hillocks and humps of the 'ant-hills' everywhere. In an intricate subterranean kingdom the massive queen breeds ceaselessly until, no longer fecund, she is licked to death. The 'workers' that kill her also fetch each colony's foodstuff of dead wood and straw, while 'soldier termites' with poisonous glands attempt to ward off aardvarks, and 'fishing' chimpanzees. Weaver ants 'sew' with silk spun by their larvae the leaf nests sometimes seen at Abuko.

The Gambia has over 30 species of snakes. (Invariably, though, they hear one coming and prefer evasive action.) The African or Rock python has been so hunted for its twenty-foot skin that only

Warthog, termite mound and Spotted hyaena at Abuko

Nile monitor

small numbers survive, far from man. The shorter Royal python is so called because of its distinguished markings, but merits more the nicknames of 'Ball python/Shame snake'. Attacked or just approached, it betrays its stately looks and asphyxiating strength: it rolls into a ball with its head hid in the middle. Though easily found by the specialist, most snakes thus show a discreet, considerate dread of the equally timorous visitor.

Yard-long 'iguanas' (grey-green and yellow Nile monitors) are glimpsed in riverside clearings or fighting the current across. (The swimming sinuosity also seen is probably not a Smyth's Water snake but the 'Snake-bird', the African darter.)

Agamas, at their best in irridescent orange and blue, more often sandily drab, are the homely and ubiquitous lizards which bask in hotel gardens. Unless one moves smoothly into their circular field of vision, they scuttle off jerkily up walls. Outside walls, I should add. Inside, and even upside down on ceilings, their smaller relatives are geckos.

On sale at the 'roadhead' by Kartung are splendid specimens of the ten-inch *Cymbium glans*, the 'largest of the genus and the most graceful', with grains of sand trapped in its salmon-pink glaze; of spiny-whorled *Hexaplex* and *Murex senegalensis*, vermilion inside when taken alive, colourless (like all shells) when collected dead. Birds are here as fond as anywhere of the common cuttle-fish – not a fish, but the skeleton of the squid. The half round, half serrated 'sand dollar' seen on beaches is the skeleton of the sea-urchin. The Gambia's cockle-shells even make a versatile building material: mixed like aggregate with bitumen for roads, set decoratively in concrete for the Palm Grove's paths and benches, used as insulation on the Sunwing's roof and strewn like gravel in The Atlantic's drive and 'Citrus Garden'. Plaster and building-lime also come from burned oyster-shells. The piles stacked by roadsides, not only near Oyster Creek, are destined for this; they are not evidence of aphrodisiacs or pearls. Though despised as 'mud oysters' by hotel chefs, they make thick and tasty pickings, from the mangrove roots, for villagers and boating parties on the bolongs.

Agama lizard (above)

Oyster-shells crushed for mortar, Lamin (below)

The daily catch of molluscs, Ghana Town

On beaches and tidal flats, sand-crabs discern you, ogling with their 'eye-tufts', and scuttle for the nearest hole. Fiddler-crabs teem on the mud at low tide. Initially alarmed, reappearing just as promptly, they are recognized by their gigantic *chelae.* On the males one of these claws is even fiercer, to woo the females and warn off other males. The low-tide mud of the mangrove swamps is also home for the journalists' 'fish that breathe and climb trees'. The African lungfish was first discovered in The Gambia, on MacCarthy Island in 1835. It 'hibernates' during the tourist season, buried in riverside mud. The amphibious mudskipper is a biological anomaly seen by river-banks and bolongs, moving true to its name and even scaling the stilt-roots of mangroves.

Fiddler-crab, Kotu Strand

No visitor can remain oblivious to the brilliant abundance of The Gambia's birds, some 500 species having been reliably sighted and 277 in Abuko alone. Tea-time ornithologists can birdwatch whilst imbibing by The Atlantic's pool or from the terrace of their room. Common garden bulbuls wake them at daybreak. Red-billed Senegal Fire-finches flutter and peck under tables, Cockney sparrows of Africa but dazzlingly male-red. Pure white Cattle egrets on the Kotu Strand's lawns, the Fajara's inseparable Pink-backed pelicans, African swifts dipping over the Tropic Gardens, superb Glossy starlings and some 30 wintering species enhance most hotels' grounds.

Sandpipers and sanderlings, turnstones, oystercatchers, redshanks, greenshanks and godwits 'wade' along the water-line; plovers scurry behind the beaches while Pied crows and magpies scavenge them clean. Gulls and terns perch on groynes or bob, a white flotilla, in the waves. Gorgeous Blue-cheeked bee-eaters teeter beside Long-tailed shrikes on telephone wires round Banjul. Nearby Abuko's

riverine forest is the haunt of multicoloured rollers, sunbirds and barbets, parrots, parakeets and many other species. Weaver birds and lilytrotters live up to their name in nesting colonies and on ponds everywhere.

On any cruise up river or into a bolong, pelicans paddle lazily clear of your boat. Or, flying gracefully, land clumsily, to roost atop the tangled mangroves like the backdrop to a comic-grotesque opera. Perched even higher, superb River eagles look down on them and you. Immobile on a lower stump, Pied kingfishers suddenly plummet, wings folded back, on their prey. Ospreys catch the eye with a similar distant splash. Its plumage the colour of mud, the anvil-headed hammerkop refuses to move, trusting in the African tradition that to kill it brings bad luck. Heavy-winged herons – Black-headed, Goliath or Grey – flap off as you approach, cormorants perch with wings ajar to dry, while African darters wriggle underwater. On drives up country you flush the Double-spurred francolin: marabous and vultures near the villages may spook you.

Government. The Gambia, *pace* recent Western press reports, is an independent sovereign state. The sixteenth member of the Commonwealth and 115th of the United Nations, it is headed by the President Al-Hajji Sir Dawda Kairaba Jawara. The Peoples Progressive Party he formed (as the Protectorate Peoples Party in 1958) won the colony's second general elections in 1962 and, with internal self-government granted by Britain the following year, led The Gambia to full independence on 18 February 1965. A second referendum in 1970 succeeded (where in 1965 a first had failed) in constituting the country a republic.

The headlines that early in 1982 proclaimed the creation of a new state, Senegambia, were echoes of ideas 200 years old, but untrue. A British 'province' of that name was admittedly established in 1765, when the Gambian trading stations came to be administered from the Senegalese town of St Louis. It survived, though, only until 1783 when the Treaty of Versailles returned the latter to France. The Gambia and Senegal subsequently developed into distinct political and cultural entities, and their separate independence remains unchanged. On 1 February 1982 a Senegambian confederation came into effect: a joint parliament is projected, on the lines of Europe's at Luxemburg, and a joint foreign policy, but with each state's diplomatic links and missions left intact. Senegal will benefit through a Customs union – The Gambia's low tariffs raised to Senegal's levels will put paid to the former's busy 'transit' trade – and The Gambia, having never had an army, has the reassuring presence of Senegal's gendarmerie.

The Gambia assumed its present shape, piecemeal, in the course of the 19th century. Our knowledge of the traditional divisions (into 'kingdoms' or, more correctly, spheres of tribal influence) is steadily increasing. Though some correspond to modern administrative limits, they carried little weight with the Anglo-French Boundary Commissions that demarcated in the late 1880s the present-day frontier with Senegal. Abolishing African slavery by the Act of 1807, Britain announced a first 'Settlement of the Gambia' as a base from which to enforce it. In 1814 the fort on James Island was reoccupied but in ruins, so two years later the 'king' of Kombo agreed to cede by treaty the island of St Mary's for the building of Bathurst/Banjul. 'King' Kolli of Kataba in 1823 reacted similarly to the offer of British friendship (plus a small cash annuity) and surrendered Lemain/MacCarthy Island, and these two administrative/military outposts constituted the original colony. Brunnay, 'king' of Barra on the north bank opposite Banjul, was persuaded to yield the rivermouth's 'Ceded Mile' in 1826. 'British Kombo' (from Oyster Creek to beyond Cape St Mary) was obtained by treaty in 1840, all of Upper Kombo in 1853. The isolated French enclave of Albreda was handed back in 1857, and various similar acquisitions were the missing pieces in the colonial jigsaw puzzle which became the four divisions of the later protectorate. Both this and the colony were governed through Sierra Leone until separation in 1843. 'Independence', with Bathurst's own 'Governor/Commander-in-Chief/Vice-Admiral of the Port', lasted until 1866. Then the rule of Freetown's Governor-in-Chief was resumed, The Gambia reincorporated into the West African Settlements and the Governor's burden of office lightened to simply 'Administrator'. Although Bathurst's legislative council was revived in 1888, it was not until 1901 that a Governor was reinstated in the 'Crown Colony and Protectorate of The Gambia' – the state's official designation until independence in 1965.

The annual Opening of the Lawcourts, Banjul

The Gambia was in 1906 administratively split into five divisions which remain much the same today. Only the old South Bank Division and the 'capital and colony' of Kombo-Foni have become the Western and Lower River divisions. The North Bank, MacCarthy Island and Upper River divisions have retained their name and shape, the last two abbreviated conveniently to MID and URD. Banjul has a city council with a mayor and elected councillors. In the 'provincie' seven area councils group the 35 traditional districts which each elect a member to the House of Representatives and is each led by a *seyfo* or chief. Unlike colonial France, which installed French nationals or trusty 'natives' to rule, Britain preferred to enlist tribal worthies as agents of the central government. The hereditary *seyfolu* were thus left to judge local issues, with an *alkalu* (headman) as 'law-enforcer' . . . and still are, although to a diminishing degree.

The Gambia's name may be a mistake. 'Gambo', 'Gambra', 'Gamboa' or 'Gambea', the term had long been known to Europeans but not, it seems, to the Gambians themselves (who referred to the river as just that: *jio, dex* or *mayo* in Mandinka, Wolof or Fula). The first Portuguese explorers, according to the griots, 'landed and met a Gambian called Kambi Manneh' (or, if not that, 'Kambi Sonko'). "What is the name of this place?" they asked. "My name is Kambi", he replied. They wrote that down'. The Mandinkas' pronouncing *g* as *k* is a credible element at least.

Population. The Gambia ranks fourth amongst African states for the number of inhabitants to the square mile. This is due more to lack of square miles than to any excessive over-population. And only statistics indicate pressures which, compared with Europe's, are minute. When cows and goats have eaten the vegetation bleak or the soil's natural nutrients been drained by cultivation, there is room for the herder and the farmer to move on. Villages built of mud-brick and thatch are easily rebuilt elsewhere: since the tarmac was extended from Soma to Basse, whole settlements have upped and rehoused themselves nearer the road (making a nonsense of all existing maps). Only the wildlife is crowded out.

The last national census, in 1978, showed a total of 493,499 inhabitants, who were asked to state their tribe. They acknowledged themselves to be Mandinka, Fula or Wolof, Jola, Serahuli, Serer or Aku, Manjago, Bambara or Other Gambian. And unlike many 'progressive' Third-World countries, The Gambia just as readily acknowledges tribalism. It is not for that any the clearer. Travel writers talk of the 'slim athletic Mandinka with his fine and friendly traits', the 'tawny straight-haired Fula' and 'the taller

Waiting for the President, the Independence Day parade, Banjul (right)

In the Kombos, twin-span ox-cart on a laterite track

Wolof, generous and intelligent, with an unnegroid nose and peaceable disposition', the 'blackest of Gambians' in one writer's view, 'lighter' according to another. Generations of intermarriage invalidate such facile aids to tribal identification. Appearance, blood-ties, origins and religion have all failed to provide the ethnic missing link. While 'British Indian' or 'American Irish' indicates origins (or clan associations), 'Scot', 'Yorkshireman' or 'Cockney' general habitat (or humour), West Africa's peoples move, mix and intermarry, frustrating the experts' attempts to define. Nowadays the latter take language to be the best criterion in classifying tribes.

Only those innocent of African orthography would attempt to list them alphabetically. 'None of these peoples have any script', or at least only the marabouts' Arabic, and the compilers of the first reports were traders, explorers, missionaries and administrators. Scholarly consistency was not their forte; their spelling, like Lawrence's in the *Seven Pillars of Wisdom*, was cheerfully erratic. Mungo Park's Feloops are thus the protectorate's Floops or Felupps, *alias* the modern Jolas, Jolahs or Diolas. The Fulas are Fulahs, Foulahs or (in Nigeria) Fulani, the Mandinkas variously Mandingas, Mungdingoes, Mangdinkas or Mandingo(e)s. As for the Wolof, I am grateful to *Enter Gambia* for all the Rabelaisian possibilities: Woloff, Wolloff, Wollof, Joloff, Jolof, Jolloff, Jollof, Djolof, Jaloff, Joluff, Galofe, Yolof, Yaloff, Yuloff, Ioloff, Ouolaf, Oloff, or Oualofe. Not forgetting the Wallofs, Oullofs and the 18th century's 'Grand Jolloiffs'.

The Gambia's most numerous are those groups that speak Mande, a dialect of the Niger-Congo family of Bantu languages. Their homeland of Manding in the Futa Jallon explains the name Mandingo; their pronunciation the alternative version Mandinka. Although one oral tradition has their king Amari Sonko conquering the future Niumi and Badibu in the 7th century, Manding or Mading is known to have been founded by Sunjata Keeta 600 years later. (It is better known as the empire of Mali) (or Melle/Melli). This in 1329 overran the neighbouring empire of Jenne (whence *Guinea*). Following the traders who fetched precious salt from the coast, Mali's young men then went west as warriors, conquering an empire from Manding on the Niger as far as the Atlantic, and south

Happy mother in handsome *granbuba*

from the Sahara to modern Sierra Leone. By the 1500s Mali had suffered the fate of all empires, but the Mande-speaking kingdoms that replaced it maintained a piecemeal Mandinka 'commonwealth' in the Gambia, Senegal and Niger river valleys. In the first, Kaabu was foremost. Flourishing under the Nyancho clan as metropolitan Mali fell, it perpetuated ruling families from which many a Gambian still boasts his descent. Only recently, however, has this early Mandinka nation come to academic ken.

In 1623 Richard Jobson's *Golden Trade* reported the Mandinkas as 'Lords and Commaunders' here still. Travelling via the Gambia to Manding, Mungo Park wrote in 1796: 'The Mandingoes constitute in truth the bulk of the inhabitants . . . and their language . . . is universally understood, and very generally spoken'. Their fourteen Gambian states had been mapped by Le Sieur d'Anville in 1751. Each ruled by a *mansa* (king) and council of elders (*alkalis/alkalolu*), they survived unchanged for another 100 years until, slowly engulfed by Jolas and Fulas, they were largely demolished in the Soninki-Marabout Wars. It was nevertheless with the Mandinkas, wrote one stalwart British imperialist, that 'the English and French had chiefly to fight in their "peaceful penetration" of the Gambia and Senegal'. Any conflict nowadays is no more than electoral: the ruling PPP party is largely made up of Mandinkas, the President their most distinguished member.

The Mandinka proportion of the total population (circa 40%) is declining nationwide but increasing in the capital. This upshot of the census surprised, for Banjul has customarily been predominantly Wolof. Colonial Britain furthered the preponderance, recruiting Wolofs (alongside Akus) into the Civil Service. The preference was slightly unexpected, for although some Wolofs had fled the French annexation of St Louis in 1816, settling with/for the British in Bathurst, their fellows in Salum and Badibu were the spearhead of the Muslim revival which Britain in the mid-19th century helped the 'pagan' Mandinkas to resist.

While some trace East Africa's Bantus back to the Niger Valley, others reverse the demographic drift to explain the facial similarities between the Wolofs and the peoples of the Nile. (Whether Mesopotamia or East Africa be the cradle of mankind, the latter seems more likely.) Arab races, the 'Libyans' of antiquity, reached the Niger in the 7th century and may have sown their seeds. The Wolofs themselves stretch collective memories only as far back as Songhoi. From this 14-16th-century empire of 'Songai', 'Sanaga' or 'Sanagha' – perhaps established by Sudanese tribes and historically demolished in 1591 – comes the modern *Senegal*. There spelt usually *N'Jay*, in The Gambia *N'Jie*, the commonest Wolof family name is further evidence in favour of their claim to descend from the S*ungai*-speaking S*onghoi* colony of Gualata. Described by Cadamosto as 'Az*anaghi* or tawny Moors', the Wolofs called this homeland Gualafa, from which *Wolof* is a short linguistic step.

The Wolofs' documented history starts with the Portuguese. Colonizing southward in the 1480s, John II of Portugal gained a foothold in Sine Salum by offering to help one Bemoi against his brother Sibetah in a struggle for this 'Moorish', Muslim kingdom. Bemoi accepted the condition that he take up Christianity, visited Lisbon to be baptized John, sailed home escorted by a Portuguese fleet and, promptly reneguing, was stabbed by the admiral. Seventeenth-century privateers suppressed mutinies amongst the 'Jaloff slaves'; in 1730 Francis Moore located in the Ba Salum 'King-dom of the Grand Jolloiffs' the (still-undiscovered) Gualata. Bathurst's

Waiting for the riverboat, Bambali

Methodist missionaries found the Wolofs the most easily converted. During the Soninki-Marabout Wars, the predominantly Muslim Wolofs of Badibu and Bur Salum were decimated by their co-religionist Maba: in March 1863, 2000 refugees reached Barra Point, to rather alarm the one British constable on duty. (Outram Town, alongside Oyster Creek, was built for them and those that followed.) Few Wolofs resided hitherto in The Gambia's Mandinka kingdoms, but the half of Bathurst called Melville Town was already in the 1830s better known as 'Jollof Town'. The place-name, though changed, remains symptomatic: Banjul's population today is 52% Wolof. In 1952 they founded the United Party, mostly Roman Catholic, and the Muslim Congress Party. They remain influential in the Civil Service and outnumber others in the Sunday congregations.

The Fulas come numerically between the Mandinkas and Wolofs. Their eighteen per cent of the national total is doubled in the area of George-town, but the concentration implicit misleads. For the Fulas in general are gypsies, and even, in one French writer's flight of fancy, 'descendants of the Shepherd Kings of Hyskos, driven from Lower Egypt sixteen centuries before Christ'. With straight hair, fine thin lips and a negroid coloration that could be called *fula* (red), the pure Fulani are an anthropological enigma. Historically we know that their ancestral home was Massina and the Futa Jallon. In the latter they lived pastorally alongside the Mandinkas 'with whom they had no quarrel, but even some affinity'. Timbo or Toobah was the Fulas' Manding, the 'seat of the hierarchy' to which, 'when ... about to make war, they send ... to invoke the prayers of its priests'. Their best-known collective and authenticated action is the 16th-century Great Trek: led by one Kolli Tengella (and guided by an oracular parrot) the 'Futa Fula' moved west en masse. They established the kingdom of *Fula*dugu, gave the Buruko Rocks the nickname of Pholey's (Fulas') Pass and disseminated the *Pholeycunda* (Fula Town) found *passim* on Francis Moore's map. Spreading north and west of the Gambia valley, they were finally contained by the Wolofs and, under the Denianke dynasty, founded the kingdom of Futa Toro which survived for 200 years more.

Top speed into town, Tendaba

Playing truant, Lamin Tenda

The 15th-century Portuguese already found Fulas south of the river; their contemporaries are on record as purveyors of gold to Timbuktu. The warlords Maba and Musa Mollo were also Muslim Fulas. Born in 1809, the son of a marabout in Badibu, 'Ma Bah' became the leader of the Muslim revival: with a largely Fula force of 3000 well-armed men, he broke the Mandinkas' hold on the valley and, until his death in 1867, led the British a bitty military dance. Musa Mollo in 1875 came down from the Futa Jallon, to convert widely by the sword and found the kingdom of Fuladu.

The Fulas who (in the 1850s) moved down river to pillage (in a 'kind of annual outing', the *Official Handbook* says) were the Fulbe Futo from the homeland of Futa Jallon ('Fulbe' being the term used by some for The Gambia's Fulas in general). The Fulbe Firdu and Torodo had gone before, the Fulbe Burure followed, and their divers offspring here now form the densest concentration of Fulas in West Africa. All that these 'Gambra Fuli' have in common is their speech (nine dialects of the West Atlantic group of Niger-Congo languages) and their cattle.

While the Fulas are multifarious the Jolas are fewer and more uniform. Their one tenth of The Gambia's population is the tip of a demographic iceberg: the Jolas, Djollas, Djolas, Diolas and/or Dyolas increase in density south through the Casamance, as far as the Ivory Coast. They are thought to be the region's aborigines but of that there is no proof: Western historians share the Jolas' ignorance as to their antecedents.

The academic assumption appears to be that, as the Fulas, Wolofs and Mandinkas are known to be immigrants from elsewhere, the Jolas *faute de mieux* must have been here first. Prejudicial evidence in that direction is found in colonial reports: 'the Felopps' (Jolas) 'go almost naked ... they wear only a little apron passed between the thighs ... they cicatrize their face and body ... and are the most backward of tribes'. Vis-à-vis the Portuguese they seem to have been more forward. The 'Floops' in 1447 killed the explorer Tristan Nunes, but their later relations with his female compatriots were such that by 1700 their 'capital' of Bintang was 'chiefly inhabited by half-castes'. The Jolas were by then being forced west and south by the Mandinkas' advance. Concentrated since in the district of Foni, they are said by some to be impervious to change.

The unflattering comments of protectorate officials – 'the Jolahs are wild ... truculent ... an unsociable race, worshippers of the Devil' – seem historically unjust. In 1780 they had housed and re-equipped a British naval force trapped by the French: '400 Jolas were mobilised to prevent the French from landing and destroying the factory of a British trader at Bintang'. 'English property, of considerable value, has frequently been left' there, noted Mungo Park, and guarded by the 'Feloops with the strictest honesty and punctuality'. Though some Jolas fought as mercenaries in the Soninki-Marabout Wars, their south-bank settlements were so ravaged by Fodi Kabba that sixteen of their 'kings' begged for British protection in 1887. And when his fellow warlord Fodi Silla was fleeing the expeditionary force in 1894, they loyally refused him asylum. The Jolas' escape route from these various marauders was from Foni into British Kombo. And even to St Mary's Island where in the 1840s they already formed a separate 'Jola Town' (and came to be called 'Banyons'). In the 1900s, the contemporary Henry Reeves writes, the Jolas 'still despise clothing ... even in the streets of Bathurst'. There is no such naturism to contemplate today.

With ten per cent of The Gambia's population, the Jolas are a half per cent ahead of the Serahulis (*alias* the 'Serrahooli, Saruhele, Sarakole, Sera Koli, Serrekoli' or even, to Mungo Park's ear, 'Sierra-Woolly'). Speaking Mande, they are linguistic relatives of the Mandinkas, but of older stock. Predating Mali and Gualata, Ghana was a 10-11th-century Serahuli empire that stretched, via The Gambia, from Mauritania to the modern state of that name. It was founded supposedly by lighter-skinned Berbers who thrived on trade with their homeland of Morocco. When their empire fell to Songhoi, many Serahulis moved south. By the 1450s they were well ensconced in the north-bank Gambian district of Wuli, where the Portuguese plied them with tobacco and strong drink. The latter may be blamed for some Afro-European interbreeding; the Mandinka kingdoms all around had a similar genetic effect and, on their Great Trek west through Wuli, the Fulas left 'the inevitable traces of their passage, in the further mixing of the already confused strain'.

West Africa's upheavals in the 19th century brought further Serahuli immigration. Itinerant and enterprising, they served as mercenaries in the north-bank kingdoms and during the Soninki-Marabout Wars. Nowadays they grow groundnuts and, on their plots by Basse, The Gambia's best cotton; their womenfolk make pots in the villages near by; but the Serahulis are first and foremost traders. Their dealings enriched the original Ghana; they 'carried on a great commerce with the French in gold and slaves' and, Mungo Park continues, 'derived considerable profits by the sale of salt and cotton'. Present-day interests are vested more in Liberian diamonds and Banjul hotels. The Serahulis nevertheless still warrant Park's verdict of 'indefatigable in their exertions to acquire wealth'.

The Tukolors (or Tukurols) are usually not thought an ethnic entity, rather the upshot of Fula penetration amongst the Serers in Fula Torodo. The Bainunkas too, though aboriginal, have merged in The Gambia with Jolas and Mandinkas, retaining their collective identity and matriarchal society only outside our area in the Casamance. The only other tribes acknowledged by the census are the Serer, Bambara and Manjago. The first, according to some, are 'relics of the primitive negro race which originally occupied the coast'. They may have been pushed down to the river mouth by Mauritanian Berbers in the 10-11th centuries. The Mandinka advances that sent the Jolas south to the Casamance forced the Serers back north. They rebounded south again in the 1850s, off Maba and

Jujus round the neck, in a Tukolor
community

Bowler, pin-stripe and old school tie,
at a Banjul government function

his horde in Sine Salum. In 1863, 2000 crossed the river, to settle in Half Die
and help construct the road from Oyster Creek to Cape St Mary. Their
progeny are still found fishing on the river and farming in the Kombos.
And on the bank at Barra building boats.

Like the Fulas, the Bambaras (or Vangaras)(or Wangara/Guangaras) sold
gold to Timbuktu. Their warrings around Fuladu delayed Mungo Park and
their general bellicosity seems, obliquely, to have benefited Britain. By
repeatedly raiding Kataba for cattle and slaves, they induced its king to
surrender Lemain Island in 1823. Advancing again in 1840, they were
frightened off by British reinforcements: a grateful King Kolli signed a
treaty of friendship and commerce, ceded land to the British government
and agreed to the building of Kataba Fort. The Bambaras still seem
somehow non grata: no one appears unduly concerned that, of all the
census's tribal totals, theirs shows the only sharp decline.

The Akus are interesting folk. Far from being autochthonous, they date
their appearance in The Gambia very precisely to the 1830s. Or rather their
partial reappearance, since they are descendants of the Liberated Africans.
Britain in 1772 freed her 15,000 'negro servants' and, as a new home for 351
of their number, the Sierra Leone colony of Freetown was founded in 1787
by the Society for the Abolition of Slavery. The 'Abolition of Slaves' might
have been a better title, for these former domestics of the British aristocracy
found themselves 'deposited in good faith on … that brooding forest land
from whence their forefathers had come'. Gentlemen's gentlemen, they
were shipped to the sticks with, as their literal companions-in-arms, 60
women 'swept from the gutters of London and Portsmouth'. The unlikely
bedfellows sired a light-skinned generation which moved north to seek a
semblance of Britain in Bathurst.

Batiks and tye-die at any *bengdula* (craft market)

Meanwhile the Royal Navy, armed by the Act of 1807, was intercepting the slaving ships: French, Spanish, Portuguese and particularly Americans flying the Spanish flag. Their human cargoes were recaptured and released, for 'rehabilitation' in Sierra Leone. And whenever it was Britain's turn to control that colonial shuttlecock, Gorée, she repatriated Negro slaves from this island-entrepôt to Freetown.

'Freedmen' redirected from Nova Scotia, discharged West Indian soldiers … for the Governor of Sierra Leone this was soon too much. Since the newly built Bathurst was undermanned and MacCarthy Island in need of a greater British presence, Liberated Africans from these several sources were in 1832-38 resettled there. For British officials ignorant of both their language and their homeland, they were often 'of no known abode'. (They had in fact been taken from every coastal region and the Yoruba-speaking Akus amongst them explain the generalized designation.) The first batch of Akus, of 'English extraction', had brought with them the names of their trades or adoptive employers: Coker, Cole and Forster, Turner, Wright and Joiner-George. Later arrivals looked to the Methodist missionaries, the Señoras and the Christian Wolofs who converted and/or cared for them. (The Gambia's Spaldings, Stapletons, Kings and Grays were disseminated by West Indian soldiers stationed here.)

With a lingua franca of English, the Akus were soon assimilated more to the British administration than to the native population. Their better education in the missionaries' schools entitled them to senior positions: if Reform Clubs are bastions of the Establishment the preponderance, by 1912, of Akus in Bathurst's is significant. Their influence waned with the British Empire; self-government in 1963 swung the vote away from their Democratic Party and undermined much of their political power.

Generally intelligent and good-looking, the Akus soldier on as a valued 'Western' element. In their wondrous Creole or pidgin English, they run Civil Service departments, pray in the Anglican churches and utter unrepeatable secrets at St John's Masonic Lodge. But their numbers and distinctiveness grow less. Few present-day children play with the Akus' traditional *gesse*-masks; some fathers try to Africanize the English family name, while more and more older sisters are adopting Afro hair-styles and dress. The increasing preference of Aku girls for Muslims should mean a next generation or two just as attractive but rather less Aku.

The Portuguese deserve a mention not because they survive in any number (only Luiz Diaz de Losada & Co construct conspicuously) but because they were partly responsible both for the many coffee-coloured skins and for black Gambians named Da Silva and Gomez. Trade and evangelization were *arrière-pensées* of Prince Henry's during the Age of Discovery. But The Gambia sent back little gold, its kings were less interested in baptism than rum and, for the Portuguese settlers and crews, a more fruitful discovery was the womenfolk on shore. 'They are all married', according to Jobson in the 1620s, 'or rather keepe with them the countrey blackewomen, of whome they beget children.' The south-bank settlement of Bintang/Geregia (viz. *igereja*, the Portuguese for church) was

Male *fatara* or *jalabe*, feminine *granbubas* at a Banjul reception

Everyday dress, albeit exquisite, with or without matching head-dress

by 1700 a half-caste town. Intermarriage – influenced by local matriarchal tradition? – had by then also resulted in that mulatto phenomenon, the Señoras. Roman Catholic, Creole-speaking and united with once-European merchants in wedlock or in lucrative liaisons, they remained the influential better half of Senegambian society for some 300 years. Many early travellers acknowledged their hospitality; succouring the hapless Liberated Africans, Bathurst's first Methodist missionaries received much assistance from this unexpected quarter.

Their Senegalese sisters accompanied the French merchants attracted to Bathurst in the 1820s, where they fast acquired a reputation for ostentatious *chic*. British officials described with admiration (and clergymen with scorn) the Señoras walking out: their finery the latest Paris creations and their jewellery so abundant on their ample persons as to overflow on to maids alongside. (Though their bijous and their circumstances have long since been reduced, Banjul's Wolof women still make resplendent sights.)

After 200 years of rivalry with the French in Senegal (and despite the continuing 'intrusion' of Albreda), the British protectorate soon became the scene of a discreetly dynamic French presence. Up river, reminders are few – a French grave at Fatoto, *'Le Commerce Africain'* above a shack-shop at Albreda – but business in and around Banjul still feels a distinct Gallic impact. Joseph Maurel and Léon Prom moved here from Gorée in 1830 to set up a score of groundnut-trading stations. The firm they founded abandoned that commodity in 1978; their Banjul base was in 1981 burned down; in 1983 the cargo ships that bear their name made a last voyage up river, but 'Maurel & Prom' are still in business, supplying *inter alia* The Gambia's Renaults and Suzukis.

As the deeds to their original Wellington Street premises are signed by seven Maurels and two Proms, it is not surprising that the former should go it alone. Maurel Frères (not brothers but cousins of Joseph's) also ventured up river to buy and export groundnuts, branched into other lines around Banjul (and housed Alex Haley in their disused, yellow-brick depot at Juffure). And in 1854 one Monsieur Vermink began the *établissement* which in 1881 became the *Compagnie du Sénégal et de la Côte Occidentale d'Afrique*. The latter was simplified in 1887 to the *Compagnie française de l'Afrique Occidentale* and nowadays this 'French West Africa Company' – the centenarian CFAO – runs the well-stocked supermarkets at Banjul and Bakau. The International Bank for Commerce & Industry's out-of-line initials BICI are due to its true identity as the French *Banque Internationale* etc. Since 1984 the Kombo Beach Hotel is a flourishing link of the Novotel chain.

The impression of Frenchness is enhanced by the Lebanese. The Gambia, so history books say, was 'discovered' by a Levantine: in his *Periplus* of 450 BC the explorer Hanno reports 'an immense opening of the sea', on the shores of which he 'saw by night fires arising in all directions'. He took back to Carthage the skins of three 'gorillae ... of human form but shaggy and covered with hair who climbed precipices and threw stones'. Those eager to establish its historical credentials identify The Gambia from this questionable evidence of an estuary, the 'burning bush' (being cleared for cultivation) and baboons. Hanno, however, is now known to have deliberately misled: seeking new markets on behalf of a shrewd trading nation, he compiled his *Periplus* for the sake of a reputation, not to reveal commercial secrets to Carthage's competitors, the Greeks.

Whether or not these Phoenicians were here, many Lebanese, their direct descendants, have followed in their putative footsteps. (Until the end of World War I and the creation of an independent Lebanon, the first to arrive were technically Syrians.) Catholic, Muslim or Maronite, a 1000 or

Lebanese shopkeeper in Wellington Street, Banjul

47

more have for three or four generations been wholesaling and retailing, in three or four languages, with their famous/infamous commercial flair.

Amongst the British contingent, there is on a small scale the expected governmental legacy: the colony's Attorney-General become the late Chief Justice, and pre-independence administrative officers re-enlisted as contract or seconded Civil Servants. Gambia Airways, the airport and port, the ferries, the National Trading Corporation . . . many bodies both private and 'parastatal' benefit from British management and expertise. Development projects and aid programmes have led to a more diverse involvement: HMG's 'technical co-operation' officers include accountants, architects, economists, engineers and entomologists; others lecture, survey, nurse, anaesthetize, manage projects, process seeds and teach.

The first arriving in 1981, each volunteering for two-four years, British VSOs are active in teaching, nursing and engineering, midwifery, climatology, agriculture and school-book design. The non-governmental, non-religious rural development agency ActionAid accounts for a half-dozen Britons who since 1979 direct Gambians in well-digging, donkey-ploughing and (women's) market-gardening, funding other self-help projects and supporting rural primary schools. Save the Children in 1982 supplied a doctor and a public-health nurse for a two-year programme in primary health care. The Holy Ghost Fathers and associated Sisters are a vital Irish and Canadian element while, otherwise engaged most Sunday afternoons, the members of the Mile Two Sailing Club form beside the Palm Grove a happy patch of expatriates. They conduct mini-regattas to the sound of a portable fog-horn and help each other get their trailers bogged down on the beach.

The Gambia's other white expatriates consist since independence of a handful of brave Scandinavians who direct the hotels they built; of Germans, on and off in hotel management, in aid, car hire and the Banjul brewery, and of numerous but transient Americans. None are old hands: the Peace Corps has been here since 1967 and Berkeley Rice had by then written the Gambians' bugbear *Enter Gambia*. Like their British counterparts, most US nationals are here to aid and advise the deprived or undernourished: keen, well-organised Peace Corps volunteers, the longer heads of AID's far-reaching programmes or members of the US teams in TANGO, The Association of Non-Governmental Agencies.

Though rarely recognized as such by their white contemporaries, black expatriates predominate. Among the friendly and colourful crowds in the markets of Banjul and the settlements up river one sees Mauritanians in their long, loose, sleeveless robes off-white or blue. (Bearded and Arabic-speaking, these lean and hollow-cheeked *Nar* seem unlikely scions of the Berber races whose onslaughts forced the Serers and Serahulis southward.) Up from the south, also understanding Arabic, Nigerians sell shells in Banjul's Albert Market, strips of hide and goats' horns for mixing native medicine. The blacks that address you in excellent French are not tributes to The Gambia's foreign-language schooling but either 'strange farmers' or out-of-work immigrants from Senegal or Mali. (With the unemployment problem hardly any better here, is it the kinder climate, or the tourists, that attract?) Likewise more fluent in French, many stallholders and shopkeepers are immigrants from Guinea Bissau. Places like Ibo Town and Ghana Town speak for themselves: businessmen from Ghana run the biggest fishery, Serahuli smugglers grow rich on Liberian diamonds and, once the tourist season is over, souvenir-sellers with sufficient hard currency fetch carvings from Mali, Benin and Burkina Faso.

Sunday morning at Banjul's Catholic cathedral

Religion. The Gambia is proclaimed as predominantly Muslim, admitted to be limitedly Christian and in places tolerated as pagan. Lacking an establishment or articulate apologists, the last group – indigenous-African, tribal-traditional and undoubtedly still widespread – fares badly with official statisticians. In 1963, 29% of all Gambians claimed to be pagan. The census of 1973 dissected the population by Sex, Age, Tribe and twenty other attributes: 'Religious Denomination' was not one. As orthodox religion is known to have arrived here in the last 500 years, paganism must *ipso facto* be the region's original faith. Usually euphemized as 'animism', it long proved impervious to foreign persuasions and remains influential.

The Christian Portuguese made mostly opportunist converts: their churches at Bintang, Juffure and Tankular administered more to sailors and settlers than to local Africans. Despite papal bulls in favour of slavery, the Germans, Dutch, British and French that followed let drop any evangelical pretence and concentrated unashamedly on commercial exploitation. The creation of Bathurst and the British protectorate made for radical change. In 1820 The Gambia 'was recommended to the General Wesleyan Missionary Committee as an eligible spot'. Two years later Mother Anne-Marie Javouhey, first of the Sisters of St Joseph of Cluny, visited Bathurst and planned a Catholic mission that did not however materialize till 1849. It floundered for 50 years, most of its officiating Spiritans, Holy Ghost Fathers from France, dying of disease before the age of 40. Arriving in 1905, the Irish father John Meehan gave the mission a literal new lease of life. It was detached from Dakar in 1931, promoted Apostolic Prefecture in 1951 and in 1957 made the 'Diocese of Bathurst in Gambia'. This, *mutatis mutandis*, is now led by fifteen Irish priests and the four Gambian ordained in 1985 and '86. It consists of some 12,000 souls, the fine cathedral in Hagan Street, churches at Bakau, Brikama, Lamin and Serekunda and six mission stations up river.

In an intellectually admirable paper the Holy Ghost Fathers have assessed their past and present place amongst The Gambia's Muslim majority: educating, at their St Joseph's and St Augustine's 'local agreement schools'; training, with an agricultural college at Lamin; maintaining the dialogue 'Pro non-Christianis' and constituting 'the dynamic representative minority ... spiritually responsible for all'.

Their Anglican and Methodist fellows in The Gambia Christian Council also find 'progress slow or almost imperceptible from the conversion point of view'. And likewise apply themselves instead to education. The Methodists in 1821 rose to the call (above) and sent John Morgan and the ailing John Baker on a missionary reconnaissance. (They were, like a Quaker inquirer, recommended by the Governor to start at Tendaba, but the headman there reacted diplomatically by advising them to build near the river, 'then you can always jump into a canoe and get away'.) Bathurst's Wolofs and Akus were more receptive and, as the Liberated Africans Department settled batches of the latter up river, Brother Morgan's helpers followed in their wake. In 1822 Morgan opened Bathurst's first boys' high school; the girls' school founded in 1824 by the Quaker Hannah Kilham was taken over by a Methodist couple called Hawkins, and in 1835 the present Wesley Church was completed in Dobson Street. The educational cluster there still, the Bethel Nursery School beside the church in Stanley Street and the later, plainer chapels at Bakau and Serekunda are all tributes to the successive Wesleyans who rarely survived their tour of duty here.

Ceremonial dancing amongst Jola
Muslims

Given the part of British officialdom in the early colony, the Church of
England arrived surprisingly late. 'In fact it was only by accident that
Anglicans came to be here at all', said the Very Rev. J.C. Faye, a former
Gambian High Commissioner, minister of state and grand old man of
pious establishment politics. The padre attached to the West Indian
regiments here left when they were withdrawn, but the Bishop of Sierra
Leone responded to the Bathurst merchants' offer of a stipend and
accommodation by sending a permanent replacement in 1836. Only in
1901, however, was the Anglican cathedral of St Mary's completed. Its
wall-plaques (many older and relocated here) show that it promptly
assumed its rôle as official seat of worship. They are dedicated to
'Commandants of this Settlement', Colonial secretaries and Acting
administrators, Governors, travelling commissioners, naval captains and
constables, and almost all donated by fellow officers or indebted 'directors
and shareholders of the Bathurst Trading Company'.

The Anglicans duly contributed schools (St Mary's in 1939 and the
Parsonage Nursery) and remaining Aku-civic and close to the
establishment, they like the Wolofs entered politics at the prospect of
independence. In 1951 'Uncle' Faye founded the Democratic Party.
(Merging with the Muslims as the Democratic Congress Party, this finally
renounced its odd programme of confederation with Sierra Leone and
bowed out to the PPP in 1968.) Faye meanwhile had been headman of
Kristi Kunda: its former St John's Church and Transfiguration School was
the last, remotest outpost of the Anglicans' Upper River Mission. Their
land at Basse was half leased off to the Standard Bank, half occupied by St
Cuthbert's (a cowherd like the local Fulas). The War-time hut at Bakau was
recently rebuilt as St Paul's, a mud hut thrown up in 1945 likewise
promoted to Christ Church, Serekunda. And with St Andrew's at Lamin
and Farafenni's Church of the African Martyrs, the Anglicans share with
the Methodists half of The Gambia's Christian five per cent.

There is a Seventh-day Adventist Church in Kanifing; fetishism, we may
assume, is the solace of a far more sizeable minority but, whether
practising or putative, the Gambian majority is Muslim. They are

technically of the Sunni sect, and the Malikite school of jurisprudence is applied in the Islamic courts. This for most Gambians, though, is the *Bourgeois Gentilhomme*'s prose: at most they avow themselves members of the Senegambian Tijani and Murad communities.

The first decades of British missionary effort coincided – by chance? – with a revival of Islam. The word of the Prophet had been heard here long before, Arab armies having reached the Niger in the 7th century. The faith spread with trade, through Morocco and Mauritania to the empire of Mali: in 1324-25 one Gongo Musa performed the *Hajj* (the pilgrimage to Mecca) and resided in Cairo with such an impressive retinue as to warrant a mention in contemporary Arab chronicles. The Mandinkas' dispersal from Mali to Kaabu was no doubt a fillip to The Gambia's Islam. Except amongst the Fulas, it none the less remained the domain of a chosen few: the marabouts, 'marybuckes' or morymen, whose literacy in Arabic was useful to unschooled rulers but whose proselytes were consigned to a 'Marabout's place' or *Morykunda*. In these satellite villages they lived safe from Soninki 'contamination' but within beck and call of their Mandinka overlords.

Due perhaps to accumulated pique, perhaps to the appearance of more warlike marabouts, Senegambian Muslims in the 1850s commenced a series of bitty uprisings glorified with the title of Soninki-Marabout Wars. The warlords Musa Mollo, Maba, Fodi Silla and Fodi Kabba engaged bands of Jola and Serahuli mercenaries, plundered and displaced the Wolofs and Serers, and destroyed the Mandinka kingdoms. Such disturbances could clearly not be countenanced by Victorian Britain in a colony and protectorate. The Royal African Corps of 'blue-jackets' and marines, seconded West Indian regiments and the Bathurst Militia with enlisted

The Great Mosque, Toniataba

Village *sering dala*, with pupils and a paddle inscribed with Qoranic texts

Kenye-Kenye Jamango, a Muslim holy place

English merchants received half-hearted help from Whitehall in containing the Muslim outbreaks. The problem was partly disposed of by chasing the ringleaders into French Senegal.

The failure of this Islamic revival, the British-backed success of Soninki animism is often seen as the reason for the relaxed, pragmatic tolerance shown today by albeit Muslim Gambians. One may with impunity (and shoes removed) visit the simple village mosques and the backyard *jakas* (praying-places). The 'missionary wing' of Islam, the egregious Ahmadi sect, may slip Qorans into hotel bedrooms, but the trusty Gideons' Bible is there in the bottom drawer too. Early Friday afternoon, dressed in their Friday best, the men of every hamlet start their walk to the nearest *juma*. Prayers at the Great Mosque on this Muslim sabbath are the cause of Banjul's weekly traffic jam. But devotions are affable, not fanatical: there is nothing of the blinkered and insidious Islam that is tainting several Middle Eastern states.

Here the *pickens* sit in the village square, learning the Arabic inscribed on wooden paddles. Older brothers, before and after school, attend the local *dala* to study the Qoran, the *Hadisi* (Hadith) and the *Sungna* (Sunna), the 'gospel according to Mohammed'. Nowadays the occasional *sering dala* even teaches Arabic as a spoken language, not simply as a vehicle of liturgy like many Catholics' Latin. The marabouts, influential still, have reverted more to their North African rôle of soothsayers and purveyors of placebos. Famous morymen, often from Mauritania, pitch their marquees by the roadside in Banjul, to advise piously (for a price) and hold well-attended court like mediaeval potentates.

Such visiting celebrities charge more than the street-corner marabout for jujus. Amulets, gris-gris, the locals' *taami matu* (and derived from *joujou*, the French for toy), they are worn round every neck, arm, waist or ankle; simple bangles, the Fulas' *tafu* (neck-cloths) or scraps of paper enclosed in lockets to keep the name of Allah clean. They do not appear to be sacrosanct (Gambians hand them over or open them up on request), just indispensable. When Mr Morgan in 1822 asked his parishioners to take theirs off, they burned his Wesley Church down. On my first drive outside Banjul, three bracelets replaced the usual one on my driver's arm: he reported late, having had to see his marabout to extend his juju-cover for up country. Childless wives, unsuccessful businessmen, the sick and soldiers off to war all apply to their marabout for the appropriate charm to wear or best *naso* to drink.

The reasons given for their use of jujus are as many as the Gambians one asks. Theologians see them as indication of the African's hankering for tangible tokens of the supernatural or divine, his reluctance (or inability) to indulge in purely cerebral acts of faith. Scholars point to the Old Testament parallel of Rachel's stealing *teraphim* (jujus?) from her father, and Homer's having Ulysses wear a ribbon to keep him from drowning. Frank Catholics equate them with St Christophers on dash-boards and miraculous medals of Our Lady hung round necks. There may well be a connection: the recent renovation of the Banjul cathedral was an opportunity for the fathers to heed Rome's admonitions on the veneration of saints and remove most of the statues. But the congregation protested, turning out to light candles to such as the 'absent St Anthony'.

Those whose *balandango*-roots fail to save them from bullets rarely come back and complain; but others whose jujus avail them naught appeal to the crocodile pools. Or make a pilgrimage to the holy places, idyllic spots with venerated baobabs and pagan associations like Sanneh-

Mentering, Tengworo, Kenye-Kenye Jamango or Nyanitama-Dibindinto. Dressed in their best and accompanied by the alkalu, suppliant men and would-be mothers trek from even neighbouring states to offer up prayers, plus kola-nuts, money, cloth or a slave. They may stay for several days, sleeping in the flimsy thatched huts, sometimes refusing food and drink, their devotions unorthodox but their piety impressive.

Dress. So delightfully varied is Gambian dress that jujus might seem to be the only common item of attire. The lavishness and flair of what most Gambians wear is a revelation to first-time visitors. Only Banjul schoolchildren are brightly and literally uniform; only green (the holy colour of Islam) is not very commonly seen. For the rest, the array of fashions and shades is amazing; except amongst Banjul's bureaucracy there is no suit-and-tie or skirt-and-blouse conformity; West African apparel is an arbitrary affair.

Serer mother and child, Berending

Taking food to the fishermen, mother and papoose on Bijilo beach

Muslim men are typical in limp white skull-caps or embroidered 'pot hats'; older worthies dignified by the red fez, imported complete with black tassel, and Fulas recognizable by their conical 'Chinese' straw hats sometimes patterned with coloured sticky tape.

The weekly wash up river

Muslim elder in black *jalabe*, and in the midday sun (right)

54

Fula boy, just circumcised

To begin with what is taken off rather than put on, every Gambian boy is circumcised: in traditional tribal rituals as described in *Roots*, after lessons from a slave in manhood, morals, bushcraft and filial duty with a *kafo/lell* of contemporaries, or more often nowadays by unceremonious surgery at the local clinic. Boys coming up for circumcision can still be seen trekking in to the *dansukunda*, summoned by the *baringo* drum; being fêted with gun-fire and a slaughtered goat, griots' chanting and dancing at the *bantaba* on the actual day; skulking in the bush for a month or two thereafter, a stick in their hand, their head in a cloth and dressed in white calico dyed from the *woloo*-tree; then returning home with fire-wood and grass to reroof their neighbours' houses, sporting coin-decked and embroidered *teetuta* (juju-belts).

Muslim men share with their co-religionists everywhere the graceful and airy *fatara* or *jalaba*, a plain and practical, long-sleeved, ankle-length 'night-shirt'. The Wolofs' *waramba* ('very large') is the Mandinkas' *dendika buluba* ('right hand'): a three-piece combination with a *turki gambisara* (undershirt), sirwal-style trousers and a large matching kaftan-cloth that, holed for the head, hangs loose from the shoulders. The *turki(a)* and sirwal alone make a light white two-piece suit.

Most Christians and young men about town are 20th-century standard. (Often their only distinctive accessories are 'tea-cosies': coloured woolly hats either knitted by Ma or bought from a stall in Albert Market which sells nothing but coloured woolly hats.) Compared with their womenfolk, the men in T-shirts and hipsters or jeans are sartorial non-starters. For the ladies of the capital in particular exhibit a grace and taste to which words cannot do justice. The Señoras and Wolofs from Senegal made a dazzling impact on 19th-century settlers. The rows of boys treadling ancient sewing-machines in townships without a hospital or bar still say much for the demands of women's wardrobes. What amazes most is that so much feminine splendour should emerge from such humble shacks and shanties.

Women also wear the waramba (above), sometimes calling it *dappay/duppe* or (if Mandinka and circumcised) *dendiko*. But most characteristic of the Senegambian *femme* is the *granbuba*. The various styles are probably run up *ad lib*, but most have these general traits: a full-length one-piece, for which 'frock' is an understatement, with a high embroidered neck (in no way décolleté) and seams down either side beneath the elongated sleeve-holes; or sleeveless and knee-length with a contrasting,

Woolly hat specialist in Banjul's Albert Market

Gambian-Lebanese beauty at the Tropic Gardens Hotel

full, long skirt; the same length but with ebullient Marie-Antoinette sleeves and a matching, straighter skirt; with these 18th-century sleeves on a hip-length blouse and a straight skirt below, or the above in any conceivable combination. All are usually topped by a matching head-dress. And modelled by the dolls sold on the beach. About the house viz. compound, town and country women wrap a *pagne* around the waist in sarong or khanga-fashion, with or without blouse and bra.

The ladies' hair-styles, like their attire, is just as predictable as feminine taste. Whilst 'pure' Fula women have long unnegroid hair, those in Banjul with similar inclinations must resort to *défriseurs*. The supermarkets do good business with their various brands of 'Hair Straightener for Natural Frizzy Hair'. It would in this connection be unkind to point out that Mungo Park's paragraph on local hair-dos leads straight on into thatching. It would also be wrongly unflattering to add that, boating through the mangrove swamps with certain styles in mind, you might find the pattern of the air-roots *déjà vu*. Helped out by the hair-pieces sold on Banjul pavements, decked out in coins, seeds, beads and knick-knacks of plastic or bone, Gambian girls construct coiffures that are often tonsorial feats.

Fajara craft market

Called in Wolof *mussor*, in Mandinka *tiko*, the head-dress is often a work of art. (Or more prosaically, to quote Mungo Park, 'a bandage ... wrapped many times round, immediately over the forehead'.) Ribbons may be added, gold thread entwined and shells inserted. Solid gold earrings, in distinctive half-moon, wheel-rim shapes, are the family savings worn by Serahuli women. The head-dress is in places a cosmetic necessity: where washing water is precious and fetched from afar, women crop their hair short or shave it hygienically off.

In a ceremony beside which christenings pale, eight-day-old Gambians are named. Family, friends and neighbours foregather with small gifts; wetting a blade from a symbolic pot (containing water, soap, cotton, maize and kola), the officiating elder cuts a lock from the infant's head and says a silent prayer. Next he whispers into its ear the name its parents have chosen, then the same to the griot who proclaims it. The tuft of hair is later buried; mother, only eight days delivered, may not attend and, leaving kola-nuts and coke for his guests, father may also be hard to find, by the alms-begging griots above all. One need go no further than page 2 of *Roots* for a less cynical-realistic, more romanticized description of the Gambians' famed naming ceremony.

Bibliography and History. One finds very little on The Gambia in libraries and bookshops at home (although D.P. Gamble's *General Bibliography of The Gambia* is a thick and tight-typed volume; G.K. Hall, Boston, Massachusetts). Published works on traditional tribal structures are Charlotte Quinn's on the Mandinkas, Gamble's *The Wolof of Senegambia, together with Notes on the Lebu and the Serer* (International African Institute, London, 1957) and Patience Sonko-Godwin's *Ethnic Groups of the Senegambia* (Book Production Unit, Banjul, 1985).

Reading matter on 'The Gambia, General' is somewhat motley. The *Commonwealth Fact Sheet* is a dated *vade mecum*; expense-account businessmen's accessories such as the Economist's *Quarterly Review* are trenchantly if ephemerally topical. There are period pieces like Richard Jobson's *The Golden Trade* (1623, but republished by E.E. Speight & R.H. Walpole, Teignmouth) and Lang's *Land of The Golden Trade* (reprinted in 1969 by the Negro University Press, New York). The end-piece portrait of the frock-coated, top-hatted Henry Fenwick Reeve CMG, MICE, FRGS, FAS, ETC, ETC. typifies his *The Gambia*: a preened and humourless tome, impregnated with Victorian public school culture but dated also by its odd combination of jingoistic self-righteousness and colonial *mea culpa* (John Murray, 1912). Lady Southorn's is jollier. Her style and standpoint are those expected of the wife of a colonial Governor (Sir Wilfrid Thomas Southorn hangs, slightly peaky-awkward, in the National Museum) but she like many others flounders in the quagmire of Gambian history (George Allen & Unwin, 1952). Two years before the Southorns arrived, Rex Hardinge visited and wrote *Gambia and Beyond* (Blackie, 1934). It is also rather spiffing and pith-helmet, but altogether lighter weight, more 'Africa and Me'. A cut above all these, and a class apart, is *Enter Gambia, The Birth of an Improbable Nation* (Angus & Robertson, 1968). In this the American Berkeley Rice depicts the country on the point of independence with a stylish hilarity that almost stays the course. And with a warmth and affection that Gambians tend to resent.

The bulk of most general books is taken up by history. It is not unfair to say that they tell half the story badly. For The Gambia's past, like affairs of state, is 'internal' and 'external'. The former, almost entirely oral, finds little place in European archives. It is the preserve of the elders and the griots, members of a hereditary caste who, accompanied by music (and according to Alex Haley), can narrate for three days without repetition their tribe's generations of families and clans, their kings, warrings, triumphs and catastrophes, their years of abundance and seasons of drought.

These *jalis* are no doubt important. Attached to each headman and king, they traditionally precede him on his travels, and are popular features on Gambian radio and Senegalese TV. Griots, however, misled Alex Haley to Juffure, and in her study of the Mandinka kingdoms – absolute griot domain – Charlotte Quinn found their 'tales … less valuable … than the traditions and memories of nonprofessional informants'. Oral historians regard the better griots as we would good historical novelists, and give more credence to village elders and 'tarikas', the Arabic *tarikh* (history) written by the 'Mandink-Moros' of early Muslim families like the Cissays and Tourays.

These are the sources of The Gambia's 'internal' history, which Western records ignore almost entirely. Not featuring in travellers' reports or governmental archives, the historic Gambian kingdom of Kaabu has only just been 'discovered'. 'Only in the last ten-fifteen years', writes Winifred

F. Galloway, 'have oral traditions become "respectable" in western scholarly circles.' They have been a subject of academic study for scarcely any longer, and the task that faces researchers is awesome. French *universitaires* paved the way in Senegal; in Banjul's Oral History & Antiquities Division, B.K. Sidibe and the American Dr Galloway spent months tape recording the elders and griots. They translated and, by collating, sifted the verbal grain from the chaff, academic detective work which permits the piecemeal reconstruction of the nation's past.

Meanwhile one is left with 'external' history books. It is not surprising that those used in schools tend to bypass The Gambia entirely. For outside the field of slavery, European doings in West Africa had little impact on the international scene. Here one sees the tactics, not the strategy of empire: four centuries of sporadic sorties and settlement, colonial in-fighting with its *ad hoc* campaigns and expeditions. The standard histories are not best-sellers. The doyen (by default) is J.M. Gray with his *History of The Gambia* (Frank Cass, 1966). Having laboured conscientiously in official archives, this former Chief Justice of The Gambia details European relations from 1455 until 1938; but his 500 pages of meticulous minutiæ are presented pell-mell; in the welter of petty events it is difficult to see the historical wood for the trees.

A same-named book by Harry A. Gailey, Jr., being shorter, sins less in this direction (Routledge & Kegan Paul, 1964). It is written, however, in pseudo-learned Americanese that few Britons find pleasing reading. Its sub-title *An Official Handbook* sums up F.B. Archer's *The Gambia Colony and Protectorate* (Frank Cass). Reprinted in 1967, it was written in 1906, when its lists of enactments, tax returns and personnel, like its far more readable chronological narration of events, stop short.

Dresses and dolls at the Cape Point craft market

Currency.

Pre-colonial Gambia gave an interesting twist to monetarism by having as its legal tender bars of iron, salt, beads and shells. The first were from the 15th century on the mode of payment for slaves. In an early colonial cartel, English and French slavers agreed not to exceed '40 iron bars per head. (The French, however, broke their word and paid as much as 70 or 80 bars' per slave.) Planning a penal colony for Lemain/MacCarthy Island, the House of Commons in 1785 offered its king an annual rental of 30 iron bars. (The price of St Mary's Island *qua* Banjul was 103 bars p.a.) As was standard with gold, the commodity came to be used as currency in nominal not actual quantities: 'Two pounds of Gunpowder ... 100 Gun-Flints ... an Ounce of Silver is but a Barr', wrote Francis Moore. Other sinews of commerce were salt, that delicacy of Africans inland; self-explanatory Trade beads, made mostly in Venice (and still found half buried on James Island), and liquor, the exchange value of which increased in the course of its consumption.

Coinage started in the 1870s with French five-franc pieces (from which, for change, slivers were clipped off the edge). In 1892 Lagos's African Banking Corporation, and in 1894 the Bank of British West Africa began to replace them with British coins and repatriate to London the 'redundant' silver. The penny was introduced in 1907, a tenth of a penny too. The halfpenny followed in 1911, and in 1913 the once-familiar florin, shilling, sixpenny and thruppenny bits. Though many stayed faithful to the five-franc coins, one-pound, ten- and two-shilling bank notes were supplied by Waterlows in 1917. The West African Currency Board celebrated self-government with new notes in October 1964; new coins marked independence, likewise belatedly, in November 1966.

Bakau's batik market

Handicrafts here are a thriving cottage industry. Authentic, attractive and still little known, they represent extensions into tourism of ancient caste-occupations.

A 'lower' caste, paradoxically, provides the greatest craftsmen. Formed in 1970, the Gambia Gold and Silversmiths Society groups 500 men of the Chem, Job, M'Bowe, Nyang, Touray and Wadda families. Boys, never girls, are 'apprenticed' to their fathers at the start of adolescence. They begin with six grams of silver for a ring, progress through solid or hollow *argent massif* and graduate to filigree. With the finest rolled gold or silver webbed on a frame like the veins of a leaf, The Gambia's filigree masterpieces are models of the art. A rolling mill and draw-plate with holes of different sizes nowadays facilitate this fineness: older hands used a home crucible to mould their gold and silver which was then hammered and rolled even thinner. Another technique I had not met elsewhere was the 'rough-cast' use of *coos*: grains of this Guinea corn are set in molten ore, the whole thing fired and the coos tapped out when cold. Bijous encrusted with cow's horn, ebony or (illegal) ivory are more 'ethnic' but equally magnificent. The silver and gold imported from London, Dakar or Ghana go also into pendants, earrings and brooches; letter-openers and articulated fish; exquisite miniature masks and filigree fishing-boats nine inches high. There are massive silver anklets like Beduin bangles, necklaces knotted in clove-hitches and bracelets tressed like hair. Three-dalasi armbands of copper, brass and iron (which are engraved to order) are cheap contrasts to silver nuggets dipped in gold.

Wood-carving is the preserve of the Janha, Lobeh, N'Jie, Sarr and Sowe clans, and their work best inspected at the Brikama market. With the craftsmen often Bambaras or Fulas, many busts portray tribal traits: splendid pieces four feet tall and true to Fula life with three scars on each cheek, three on each temple and two in the centre of the forehead. Technically lax Muslims in this fondness for human forms, they also manufacture scale-model warriors and pipe-smoking hunters, their arrows in a quiver and an animal over their shoulder. These flank stylized

Silverware for sale in the craft market, Banjul

Rosewood Fula woman and mahogany hunter, Brikama

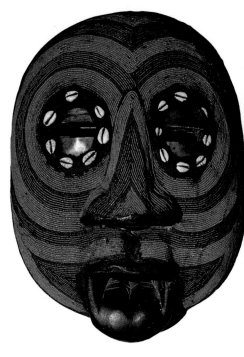

silhouettes and two-dimensional faces, but most frequent are the masks which tribal rituals require to conceal them. Some masks are straightforwardly grotesque, others draped Medusa-like with snakes, or many-faced with smaller countenances beside a 'double-decker'. Small marvels from every neighbouring state embellish many hotels; the restaurant of the Bungalow Beach has a mural gallery of boned and beaded, wood, shell and bronze wonders.

Also carved are drums, combs, paper-knives, pestles and mortars; just-recognizable elephants and 'hear no evil' monkeys; hippos and peg-men rowing salad-bowl boats; crocodiles and the same antelopes and sucking fawns that, identically stylized, appear in Kenya and even North Africa, reincarnated as olive-wood gazelles. The wood used here is mainly mahogany, the depth of its stain and shine increasing with up to five coats of brown shoe polish. (Black, they confess, is used for forging ebony.) Real ebony one tells by its weight and higher price: it is harder to work and imported from Senegal and Mali. Bowls are cheap in the Wolofs' *khankhalla*-wood; the soft 'cheese' wood of the *fromager*, bombax or silk-cotton tree is used for 'antique' statues, cracked and bleached 'with age'.

Masks from Mali, at the Bungalow Beach Hotel

Pots are a speciality of Alohungari: rotund, deep-rimmed and two or three feet wide. (The most/only photogenic views of Basse used to show them on the river-bank every Thursday morning, the *Lady Chilel* alongside.) Except on Thursdays (because of the above) and Fridays (the Islamic sabbath) the local Serahuli women work kaolin fetched from the rice paddies. It is sieved, crushed smooth in mortars and moistened for use the next day. Lacking both kilns and the potter's wheel, the women shape the clay by hand with a bowl as mould, scratch in a chevron or a crescent design (which they later outline with white paint) and fire each piece in a hollow, covered with kindling and wood.

Pots from Alohungari at the Thursday-morning market, Basse

The kora is a characteristically Mandinka instrument. Entitled to 18-24 strings, this African harp-lute has generally 21, in staves of eleven and ten. Its *keno*-wood neck and handles are held straight out, the calabash body on the performer's belly (or, if he is seated, on the ground between his knees). It is played mostly with thumbs. Whilst we beat out rhythms with brushes or sticks, using digital dexterity more for melody, these rôles are in Africa frequently reversed: drumming is a demanding five-finger exercise, while melodymakers like balafons are beaten and musical implements like 'thumb pianos' speak for themselves. Kora-players compromise, with six or eight fingers resting idle under the strings and first fingers at most helping thumbs pluck out a melody. For all that very prettily: the kora has the harp's little-bell tinkle but is less full-bodied, and the Arab *qanun's* polyphonic nimbleness but is more melodious. With captivating rhythm, even proto-jazz syncopation, its music is Indo-European mellifluous, not primitive Arab-painful. The minstrels that play it at many hotel tables complement their 60-piece repertoire with instant lyrics in one's honour. (The 'sound-holes' in the resonator-body are for notes: coins clank embarrassingly.)

The bolon or bolonbata is a lesser bent kora, with a maximum five strings tuned to the arpeggio. The *keno* neck is curved while this redwood is still green; the body is a smaller gourd, likewise covered tight in cowhide but with the hair left on. It is played only by Mandinkas, Fulas and the odd Guinean Susus (and not made any more tuneful by the large metal rattle round its neck).

The balafon is Africa's xylophone (a gift of the devil, Mandinka griots say, to the Kuyateh families in Sunjata's time). Its sound is admittedly not heavenly, more the hollow beauty of Japanese bells. With gourds hung in a frame beneath, its 16-19 keys are struck in resonant and skilful unison. The griots' balafon often accompanies the slightly nasal singing of lady griots, who accompany themselves with a *newo/karanyango* (iron bell).

The villages near Basse also produce shallow platters, globular bowls and holed coos 'cullenders'. In hamlets like Jifarong, laterite pots lie beside the track awaiting transport. Shaped like squat and irregular Mister Men, they have matching half-pot tops.

The inside rotted by soaking in water, the skin dried wood-hard in the sun, the calabash/gourd provides several rural receptacles: spoons and ladles from smaller 'stemmed' fruit split in two, and ample half-gourd bowls, often carried on heads and branded in black patterns.

The commonest wind instruments
are unfortunately football whistles.
The three-holed transverse *tabiru*
and the *serndu* of the Fula *gawulo*s
('musicians') are used in tribal
ensembles. Or to call cows. Serahulis
call *fuleh* the shorter bamboo oboe
which they play with four fingers
and sometimes cover with leather.
The Wolofs are short of wind
instruments.

Marking time for dancers,
wrestlers or working parties, whistles
are blown (and armlet *lala*s rattled) by
players of the all-important drums.
The highest in pitch is the Wolofs'
sabar, which Mandinkas call *sabaro*.
The *bellengo* is their big bass drum.
Also banged with the right hand, a
drumstick in the left, the *kuturiba*
and *kuturindingo* are the large and
small *kutur*s. They are long, conical
and leaned on. The Wolofs sit on the
ground to beat the barrel-shaped
gorong between their knees, while
the Jolas' wood-frame of 'kettle-
drums' can only be played standing
up. Called *bugarabu*, they are sets of
four – differently pitched *tumba*s plus
a larger *funyundum*. (Smaller, similar
*wimpau*s sent messages to the dead.)
The time-honoured beat of the
tabulo/tabala took news from place to
place; nowadays this bowl-shaped
drum generally waits for prayers or
funerals in each village mosque. Only
when new Mandinka kings were
crowned was the two-foot *junjungo*
beaten, *en bandoulière*, with a ten-
inch stick. At the other extreme is the
bombolo, a skinless 'idiophone' from
simply a split log. Fill the same with
jujus and the boom of this *kumba
demba* would keep Mandinka
villages safe from war or fire. The
Wolofs' *kheen*, the Mandinkas'
daaba would announce kings or send
special news: bulletins were limited
to an hour or so because thereafter,
like the kora's strings, the drum-skin
lost its tone. (Numbers performed
during European tournées may last
only fifteen minutes: in the colder
climate skins and strings sag faster.)

The Gambia's dancers are re-
nowned for their dynamism,
rhythmic flair and acrobatic finesse,
the finest exponents of 'choreo-
graphed ritual' being the Gambia
National Troupe. Their forte is the
masked or 'social' dance. The latter
may represent the Cassankas' palm-
wine 'harvest home', the Balankas'
'warring' to the popular tune *Mama*

Jola playing the *bugarabu*

Dancing-girl of the Gambia National
Troupe

The Gambia National Troupe performs at Bijilo bantaba

Manneh; Serahuli women working in paddies by moonlight or, with knives thrust symbolically and pelvises suggestively, the Jolas enacting a former forced marriage. The irrepressible Fulas that perform fakir-like in hotels are not the circus 'fire-eaters' one knows. Bundles of flaming grass they pass casually over chest and abdomen, under their chin and down their arms, to swallow them or slowly stamp them out. The 'musical accompaniment' of half-gourd *horde*-drum, awful *riti*-fiddle and side-blown *serndu*-flute would be second string to anything, let alone this.

The Jolas' *kumpo* is a startling masked dance. Preceded by a woman whose whisk and water-sprinkler cast protective spells on the circumcised and virtuous, a guide leads in the chanting exorcist. Decked in four sleeved rings of raffia, this kumpo will break the enemy's spell. In a final whirling crescendo of dust he pivots invisibly on a head-pole, his body unseen and the scene unbelievable.

Wrestling remains the national sport. *Nyoboro* in Mandinka, *boreh* in Wolof, its modern form derives from a deep-seated Senegambian tradition that probably originated in 13th-century Mali: that of the warrior, who was accredited with powers both physical and spiritual and who ranked in the tribal caste-system directly below the ruling families. (Present-day wrestlers aspire to and often attain similar social status.)

This may explain why, magnificent village he-men, they strut, dance, spar and literally play to an appreciative gallery on the breeze-block seats. Water from the second's bucket makes fine bodies slippery and hard to grip; sand on the hands improves the hold; muscles are flexed, loincloths girded and jujus buckled on before each fight. Between the bouts a woolly-hatted retinue blows whistles and bangs drums, Fulas play flutes, Jolas mouth music and the girls chant to cheer-leaders in Mandinka villages. A lap of the krinting-fenced compound in a triumphal jog-trot (and a coin collection) follows. Fingers tapped on foreheads or drawn across throats taunt or threaten. Mock biting off of genitals from a thrown opponent is less frequently seen but of deeper Black African significance: only by possessing his predecessor's penis could, for example, a Baganda claim Kampala.

There is nothing of the protracted Western business of arm-, leg- or head-locks, technical throws, falls and points. The first one down loses. Full stop. One wrestler challenges another, sensibly from the same heavy-, middle- or light-weight class and usually from the same tribe, since 'mixed' fixtures are unusual. Scorning a challenge at first may lead in the end to a more ferocious clinch: round the waist, neck or knee but often first of all on the juju-decked loincloth. Pulled, twisted, tripped or lifted bodily, one of the wrestlers soon hits the dust. Punching, kicking, biting, flinging sand in eyes or poking them is permitted but not cricket: in traditional village fixtures it will be stopped by the griot or the offending *kafo*'s 'manager', by self-appointed referees elsewhere, while the crowd boos disapproval.

Banjul. The Gambia's capital still appears often as 'Banjul formerly Bathurst'. To be precise, 'and formerly Banjul or Banjole' should be added, since the island leased by Britain in 1816 was already known as *Banjulu* to its shifting population of foragers, criminals and runaway slaves. Explanations of the name are at variance. The Portuguese who misquoted Kambi Manneh 'found the islanders cutting raffia-palm: "What is this?" they asked. They were told *banjulu* … and wrote that down'. This, the griot Fabala Kanuteh's account, differs from everyone else's: that *Banjul* means Bamboo, once found here in profusion and first cut by one Madiba from Bakau, who consequently acquired the nickname Madiba Banjol. (The local Mandinkas circumvent the problem with their *Kunu-su-joyo*, Bird's nest Island.) In 1973 the authorities dropped the name which, like that of the town in New South Wales, had honoured Henry, 3rd Earl of Bathurst, Colonial Secretary from 1812 to 1828 and son of 'the weakest though one of the worthiest who ever sat on the woolsack'.

Though birds are still abundant, bamboos and raffia-palms soon made way for an expanding township. Having acquired the site for 100 Spanish dollars (viz. 103 iron bars) per annum, Captain Alexander Grant set his 80 men to clearing the bush and building: with timber from the mainland, rock from Dog Island and mortar from burned oyster-shells. Controlling the river mouth against slavers, attracting merchantmen with its sheltered deep-water berth, Bathurst grew steadily into a loose-knit conurbation. Its hamlets, separated by plots on which 'some sickly vegetation seems to be doing violence to the poverty of the soil', were mostly self-explanatory. The half-caste Portuguese Town; Soldier Town housing the 2nd West Indian Regiment seconded to Grant's Royal African Corps; the better-class 'Jollof'/ Melville Town, Jola Town and the Moka/Mocamtown that became Half Die … all flooded indiscriminately at spring tide and during the rains. 'The people catch fish in the middle of the streets … and occasionally a crocodile … makes its appearance.'

With the Liberated Africans came the first drainage in 1832. A dyke was commenced around Half Die

Bedford Place, Banjul; buildings in 'colonial corrugated-iron style'

and in 1846 a lock at Malfa Creek; incomplete and insufficient, they were supplemented in 1862 by the sluice gates called Box Bar. An embankment was pushed south from Clifton Road, but only with the present Bund Road in place did the capital become watertight. A start was made also on the open sewage system to be flushed by each high tide. In the mid-1950s the whole thing was reversed but, with the outflow still often merely theory, not only sensitive visitors will welcome the commencement in 1984 of a new sewage system funded by the EEC.

Flooding, the surrounding swamp and motley immigration were the frequent causes of disease. Wesley Church plaques from 1837 result from 'the epidemic, which so awfully raged at that time'. Half Die is a numerical reminder of the cholera of 1869. The control effected by British officialdom was quite as much sanitary as military. Barracks built alongside MacCarthy Square grew into the governmental Quadrangle; the hospital commenced in 1853 (and ridiculed by Burton in 1863) was finally improved after 1903 with the help of the Sisters of St Joseph. Around MacCarthy Square and along Marine Parade, building proceeded in 'West African colonial' style: a nondescript (hot and unhealthy) ground floor fronted by imposing double stairways; a smarter upper storey, sometimes projecting and supported by wrought iron, and always surrounded by a colonnaded balcony; walls often whitewashed, and peaked roofs everywhere of corrugated iron. Intrinsically ugly, sheets of the last are worked ingeniously and with unusual style into spires and minarets on richer village mosques, into curving roofs and gabled dormers on Banjul's older buildings.

The latter constitute almost all of its architectural assets. On its low-lying island, the capital keeps a low profile: the Central Bank is as yet the only skyscraper and landmark. Though the Serekunda conurbation is bigger than Banjul, and Fajara far smarter, Britons at least should have a soft spot for a capital planned around a cricket pitch.

The Victoria Recreation Ground in Banjul's MacCarthy Square

The façade of Albert Market was in 1983 reworked and its original plaque removed: 'Commenced May 1854 Completed May 1855'. This emporium of tight-packed local colour begins with trays of watches and sunglasses, perfumes, toiletries and 'Special Gunpowder' China tea. There follows an increasingly exotic array: Chinese platters of oranges and bananas, coconuts, necklaces and tresses of black hair, open sacks of sugar and fancy groundnut soap. These are the last familiar objects amidst the bewilderment of unknown shapes and smells. Bowls of green *fulano* powder are mixed with water to daub on hands and feet; orange resin chunks end up as starch. Incense is burned from obnoxious black balls or a *churayi santang* mixture of seeds; tea made from bundles of the Wolofs' *mburmbur* leaves. 'Medicines' they brew from dried shoots of *kanifingo* and the fruit of the *sito* (baobab). Leaf-covered sacks contain precious kola-nuts: yellow, pink and bitter, shaped like shelled Brazils, they are chewed as a stimulant, offered to deities and/or appreciated as a tip.

Familiarity returns with Trade beads and hair straighteners as one proceeds to the central vegetable section. Stalls of salt and pasta, sunflower-seeds and Maggi cubes precede the meat and fish market behind: a malodorous display of local species, with fish scales falling thick like autumn leaves. An alley of smoked fish is an even more fulsome reason to move on, between the balls of black soap and stands of Chinese tinware, to the 'tailoring department'. In a vast hive of activity like a 19th-century workhouse, rows of sewing-machines are treadled beside their adjuncts of cloth, buttons, buckles and thread. The last alley is leather bags and shoes; sandals have soles cut from old rubber tyres. With carved masks, jewellery, ghee and twisted ginger-root as final curiosities, one re-emerges into Russell Street.

Albert Market, Banjul

The Gambia National Museum is worth an early visit: not as cultural preparation for Banjul but as an introduction to Senegambian rites and tribal lifestyles which, on a short visit, one would otherwise at most only glimpse. Of the three levels, well captioned, and with welcome ceiling fans, the entrance hall is tribal-homely: 'Domestic Life' is cooking utensils, tools for crushing cassava, and soap made by baking in the sun a mixture of palm-oil, groundnuts and ash. 'Products of Smithery' include scabbards and an aluminium elephant. 'Agriculture' is the predictable implements (*inter alia* for planting rice and tapping palms for 'wine'), 'Tanning & Leatherwork' the preserve of artisans which the Wolof call *ude* and the Mandinka *karanke*. Also a male domain, 'Spinning & Weaving' displays looms, distaffs and shuttle-boats, tie-dye techniques and Fula cotton cloth.

More exotic/erotic are 'Traditional Kingship' (*chonoo/chorno*-staffs 200 years old, symbolically male and female and which 'may also serve as a weapon') and 'Beadwork', first known 12,000 BC and here principally for initiation and fertility. This last is apparently so great a preoccupation as to warrant two displays: the 'Cult of Maternity & Procreation' is evidenced by symbolic crocodiles, tortoises and snakes (hornbills too, since their couples fly inseparable), while 'Symbols of Initiation, Maternity & Female Fertility' feature beads and calabashes held by 'women who wish for children' and dolls which (as sub-stitute or inspiration?) are 'carried by the infertile'. (Barren village women formed a class apart, called *kanyalang.*)

After masks as part of 'Traditional Warfare'; *fanals* (model boats) paraded at Christmas and New Year, and boards for the game of *bau* played since prehistoric times in Africa and Arabia, one moves to the area downstairs: bows, arrows and bee-hives hung in trees; earthenware incense-burners and cullenders, knobbly water coolers and twin-spouted medicine pots; calabashes decorated for marriages; wickerwork with which to fish or winnow; guns, spears, traps (and jujus) for hunting, shooting and fishing, and many of

Batik kora-player

the musical instruments already described.

The objects, if not the subjects, are more familiar upstairs: prehistoric tools, weapons and other flint monoliths, stones for slings or hammers and Neolithic pottery. Found locally, they resemble Neanderthal but, as the notice admits, 'it is not possible to tell whether . . . they were made at some later period'. Of unquestioned antiquity, the Senegambian Stone Circles receive the attention they merit, but are in no way explained. Further displays describe and/or illustrate shell-mounds, earth-tombs and Iron Age village middens (viz. rubbish tips); the 10-11th-century kingdom of Ghana; the Manding empire (with prints of warriors, griots and masseuses) and the 'Coming of Islam' (with Qorans, inscribed stones and a misplaced leopard skin). One far corner is devoted to the Soninki-Marabout Wars, the other to the colonial period (plans of James Island, maps and rates of exchange, Portuguese and Holland beads, and 'Manchester goods' traded for slaves). The kingdom of Kaabu has a fittingly central display, but its exhibits are of peripheral interest, and face an incongruous Queen Elizabeth II. The insignia 'EIIR' is the reason why the ceremonial silverware and china were removed from State House to a showcase here.

Beside a tiny gallery of royalty and colonial governors, the exhibition is brought up to date by an alcove 'Independence to Confederation', which includes pictures of the pilgrimage to Mecca, Harold Wilson and Mao Tse Tung.

The Banjul-Barra ferry was modernized in 1978-79. To replace the wooden *Barra*, *Bakau* and *Bulok*, the modern steel *Banjul* and *Niumi* arrived from the Germersheim shipyards on the Rhine. Custom-built to connect with the two new terminals, they cannot be used elsewhere. (And, because of a technical oversight, cannot on occasions be used even here: ferry and terminal are incompatible at certain states of the tide, so all fall back on the original *Barra*.) Embarking at the Wellington Street terminal, one is piped off by a cacophony of whistles, to enjoy a half-hour of dolphins plunging their way up river and boys with cinema-usher trays of cigarettes, rope-platters of kola-nuts and Chinese bowls of hard-boiled eggs and Juicy Fruit chewing-gum.

Boarding the Banjul-Barra ferry

Barra at first sight is all groundnut installations: the evacuation belt along a lengthy pier, lighters, lorries and the wire-fenced compound of GPMB 'bins'. But taxis also clamour for fares on to Dakar; Serers build boats on the bank and, a half-mile seaward, Fort Bullen is unmistakable. With police station and as many garages as shops, this odd assemblage is all that remains of the 'kingdom' that featured so prominently in The Gambia's pre-independence history. Christened *Barra* by the Portuguese, Niumi ('the Coast') controlled the lower river: European well-being, first at James Fort and later in Bathurst, depended to a large extent on the (proffered or enforced) goodwill of its rulers.

Fort Bullen. The colonial joke that The Gambia's borders were dictated by the range of Britain's gunboats on the river was an evident nonsense already in 1816 when Bathurst was built: its Six Gun Battery and other pieces could not cover even the river mouth and extra fire-power was required on Barra Point against the slavers still trading with Albreda. This the rulers of Niumi had refused, fearing that such guns could be used against their stronghold of Essau. But in 1823 Brunnay/Burungai Sonko came to power; in 1826 HMS *Maidstone* showed the flag together with the *African*, the first steam vessel seen on the river; the Governor proposed an annual £100 subsidy and – frightened, enticed (and habitually drunk) – Burungai agreed to the north bank's 'Ceded Mile' and the fortification of Barra Point. Two cannons were brought across from Bathurst and installed; discharged soldiers and liberated slaves soon settled alongside in the mud-hut Berwick Town. Named after the commander of the intimidating *Maidstone*, Fort Bullen saw action for the first and last time during the so-called Barra War.

Receiving missionaries 'drinking rum from . . . a tea-kettle', chasing the French Resident at Albreda back to Bathurst, Burungai so mistreated British traders in the Ceded Mile that his subsidy was suspended in 1830. The following August a drunken brawl at Barra led, by mistake, to the sounding of the alarm. Soldiers, ships' crews and civilians

Fort Bullen and Barra beach

hurried across from Bathurst and misguidedly marched on Essau. Burungai's Mandinkas, forewarned, forced them back to their boats at Fort Bullen, killing, even decapitating over 30 Britons. Panic rallied the colony's inhabitants; the French moved in from Albreda for protection; 'all, who could carry arms, were drilled and enrolled in a militia; a strong stockade was erected across the island . . . and . . . even the native women and children carried stones for the construction of a new fort'.

Coming to the rescue from French Gorée, Commandant Louvel of the *Bordelaise* first co-ordinated this defence effort and in September, with men of the West Indian Regiment, sailed for Barra. But despite the traders' formation of the 'River Fencibles' and the despatch by Governor St Germain of more troops from Senegal, the Anglo-French force was still too small. Only on 5 November 1831 – when one British commander had been dismissed, another suffered a nervous breakdown and most of the French been recalled – did Freetown's *Plumper* and *Panchita* arrive with sufficient troops to retake Barra Point. Repeated bombardment and (when the ammunition ran low) hand-to-hand fighting finally induced Burungai to surrender. On 5 January 1832 his people 'publicly declared their sorrow for the outrages . . . committed in an unjust and cruel war'.

Transit camp in the 1860s for the Muslim refugees from Maba, Fort Bullen is not on record as having been manned after 1870. Except during World War II, when the 1st Coast Battery took up positions against the (never fulfilled) menace from Vichy-held Senegal.

While these various actions are well documented, no one seems to know when the fort was actually built: 64 paces by 46, circular bastions on each corner and embrasures twelve by 24 on the firing-step of its brick or laterite-block walls. Standardly inscribed with the royal *'GR'* and William Carron's 'WCᵒ' hall-mark, cannons litter both the fort and the grounds of the hydromet station alongside. World War II counterparts rust on the beach, their emplacements on the bastions. Fort Bullen is embellished neither by the lighthouse atop another bastion nor the 'Contents of Magazine' black-stencilled in the British-army blockhouses below.

Berending. Beyond the Serer 'boatyards' and their *jaka* on Barra beach, the laterite track forks round the magnificent baobab of Essau, a rust-red (or dust-red) hamlet that is the Mandinkas' *Yesseu*, 'Throw yourself' (into the river?). Compensation for the corrugations on through Sami and Taiba is the riverine scenery of the Jiffet Bolong and the Berending crocodile pool. The attraction of the hollow is not so much its namesake *bere n'ding* (small stone) as the riverine greenery of the small pool and the lattice of air-roots that edge it. Someone soon materializes to show the way to the burrows of the tight-palm coppice in which the sacred crocodiles repose. He should be one of the Sonko family, descendants of Burungai and owners of the area. It was discovered, so they say, by Sumar Bakary and Fodi Brama, Sonko brothers who lie buried where the women now wash. Berending's supernatural properties, and its pilgrims' wash-and-drink rituals, are like Katchikali's and Kartung's, the only difference being that, if anyone in Berending is due to die by night, the crocodiles all cry the day before.

The sacred crocodile pool, Berending

Dog Island, when one sails out from Banjul, is the first perceptible feature as the river narrows into far-bank visibility. So named because of the barking, dog-faced baboons that greeted early sailors, the name was changed to Charles Island by Major Holme's soldiers in March 1661. Within a year they numbered 119 (although only 47 remained fit for duty) and James Island (then manned by only 29) still took second place in the empire-builders' thinking. Its vulnerability to the mainland at low tide induced Britain to abandon the island in 1666. One year later Duke Jacob of Courland disregarded the danger and established a garrison, whereupon the 'natives made a surprise attack and cut all the Courlanders' throats'. The same fate befell the Frenchmen whom one Captain Ducasse sent ashore to found a trading station in 1678. Eclipsed by James Island, the place served thereafter only as quarry and sanctuary: the British, by the king of Barra's leave, built Bathurst with Dog Island rock and, during the Soninki-Marabout Wars, 200 women and children fled from Maba to be evacuated from here in the Liberated Africans' canoes. Charles Fort has wholly vanished; a legendary dragon keeps the locals at a distance; breeze-blocks behind the beach and graffiti carved in the baobabs are nowadays the only marks of man.

Waterfront, Banjul

James Island

James Island, in the language of the brochures, is the Sentinel of the Gambia River. Winifred Galloway's monograph on it is sub-titled *A Nutshell History*: the history of James Island is in fact that of the whole pre-colonial country in an albeit complex nutshell. After the Portuguese Tristan Nunes had in 1447 seen the Gambia and died, the Venetian Luiz de Cadamosto was sent south by Portugal's Prince Henry the Navigator. Joining forces with Antoniotto Usodimare, he entered the river mouth in 1455, but the crews of their three caravels mutinied at the sight of the natives' canoes. They returned in 1456 and, sailing up to Badibu, passed a small island 'shaped like a smoothing iron'. Here they buried a sailor named Andrew, whence the original 'St Andrew's Island'. The two explorers failed in their quest for the riches of Timbuktu and/or the source of the Nile, but they did make friendly contact with the rulers of Badibu

Albreda

and Niumi. Diego Gomez in 1458 continued the search for the kingdom of Prester John, an abbot of Soto de Cassa made the first conversions. But with Philip II of Spain's seizure of the Portuguese throne in 1580, the 'Portingales' in Africa became increasingly detached. Convicts and refugees from the Inquisition, Moors and Jews expelled in 1609, they proved better traders than evangelists and, sowing their seeds with useful ambiguity, left The Gambia both cash

crops from the Americas and the mulatto Señoras.

Dispossessed by Philip II, the Portuguese pretender (one Antonio, prior of Crato) fled from Lisbon to the English court, where he survived by selling the Portuguese crown jewels and 'exclusive trading rights'. In 1588 Elizabeth I confirmed his ten-year grant of the last to a group of London and Devonshire merchants, whereas James I in 1619 preferred 'English gentlemen' for the 'exclusive right of

trade to Guinea and Binney' (Benin). These odd early monopolies on speculative trade in unknown parts were often unexpectedly effective: Edward IV in 1483 prevented two English ships sailing to 'Guinea'; still in deference to Portuguese rights, Francis I restricted Frenchmen likewise in 1529 and, prior to Antonio's arrival, Elizabeth limited English ships to waters in which the king of Portugal 'hath not presentlie domaine, obedience and tribute'.

The various English 'patentees' did not enjoy such guarantees. The Guinea Company is less known for its mercantile success than for *The Golden Trade*, written by one of its ships' supercargoes, Richard Jobson. The subsequent Royal Adventurers, to whom Cromwell and Charles II

gave patents, had to contend increasingly with European free-booters. Dutchmen independent since the Spanish War of Succession; Spanish captains redundant from the same and turned privateer; merchant-sailors from Rouen, all traded along the 'Guinea coast' with little respect for exclusive rights.

Germans even appeared on the scene in an odd teutonic interlude. Since 1640 ruler of Courland (the later Baltic state of Latvia/Lithuania), Duke Jacob had received as a christening gift the island of Tobago from his godfather, James I. And needing slaves for his plantations there, he sent to the king of Niumi for a plot of land at Juffure. With this source of water and fire-wood on shore, Courlanders under one Major Fock

built the first fort on St Andrew's Island in 1651. Another was reportedly constructed on St Mary's Island (likewise leased from the king of Niumi). During The Gambia's Baltic decade, a stalwart commandant called Otto Stiel maintained such relations with the local populace that they helped him see off French and Dutch intruders, speciously entitled to Courland possessions by the dukedom's metropolitan involvement in such unlikely developments as Sweden's annexation of Poland.

German-Gambian friendship was cemented even by a visit to the Baltic of Niumi's black ambassadors. Then rudely interrupted by Britain, who in 1661 seized the island in what the Courlanders considered a flagrant, Falklands-style breach of international law. The 'Royal Adventurers of England Trading into Africa' justified their acquisition by the pretext that the island was Dutch and thus at the time an enemy possession. Their envoy, Major Robert Holmes (whom Pepys describes as 'a rash proud coxcombe'), first 'caressed and entertained' the natives of Niumi to ensure the safety of his garrison on Dog Island. Having ousted Otto Stiel and his seven remaining men and women, he established Britain's first West African outpost on St Andrew's Island. Which he renamed after James, the then Duke of York and Charles II's future successor.

By 1672 the Royal Adventurers were bankrupt, and replaced by the Royal African Company. The Company of Merchants Trading to Africa took over in 1752, and all maintained on James Island a poorly supplied and sporadic garrison of soldiers, artisans, clerks, gardeners, 'linguister'-interpreters and 'factors' in charge of the trading-post 'factory'.

France meanwhile was the scene of similar politico-mercantile, state-run speculation. With Gorée seized in 1677, the Senegalese town of St Louis became the base, and the *Compagnie Sénégalaise* the agent, of increased French activity along the River Gambia. The ruler of Niumi in 1681 relinquished Albreda to the French (for a monthly rental of four iron bars) and Britain was, during the few periods of peace, obliged to recognize this enclave until it was negotiated out of existence in 1857. A five-minute boat ride from James Island, by the on-shore wells which supplied the garrison's water, it epitomized The Gambia's live-and-let-live extension of Franco-British rivalry at home. When relations there worsened into war, as in 1689, the British would land and dutifully take Albreda. When in 1695 Monsieur de la Roque disembarked to demand a British surrender, he was 'regaled magnificently and the health of each party's respective king was drunk'. The British 'resolved to wait . . . and fight until death': the French fired two shots, the garrison surrendered.

The French destroyed James Fort, confiscated its sparse stores and arms and spiked the guns that their ships could not remove. The Treaty of Ryswick having ended King William's War in 1697, The Gambia

reverted to the *status quo*. The Royal African Company rebuilt James Fort, but in 1698 lost its monopoly of Britain's 'Guinea' trade and thereby the means to maintain it. The scenario is repeated in the Spanish War of Succession, the island's ransom being the only variation. Monsieur de la Roque returned in 1702: Fort James again surrendered. His colleague however, one Captain St Vaudrille, this time offered to spare it if paid £6000. The Royal African Company agreed, but would the French accept delayed payment in three £2000 instalments? The fort, by then derelict, was rebuilt in 1703. Its garrison ('the dregs of London's taverns') mutinied in 1708 but, finding nothing worth acquiring, spiked the guns and left. With the Treaty of Utrecht in 1713 the Franco-British situation once again returned to *status quo*.

The Company reconstructed and reoccupied James Fort, to see it seized in 1719 by a British pirate, Howel Davis. 'While he was looting the island's stores, half the fever-ridden fourteen-man garrison decided to join him.' In 1725, on not 5 but 1 November, the powder-house exploded, removing part of the fortifications and eleven of the Europeans. The unedifying sequence of armed Anglo-French bickering, between Albreda and James Island, continued until 1763 when the Seven Years' War ended in the Treaty of Paris and the surrender to Britain of, not only Canada and Florida, but also all of Senegal except Gorée. The Governor of the new Crown Colony of Senegambia resided at St Louis but, because of his 'overmastering aversion to correspondence', his lieutenant-governor on James Island was left to deal as best he could with the felons sent to man the garrison. Too weak to prevent continued French slaving at Albreda, he did just manage in 1768 to hold the island against the 500 natives of Niumi who, attacking in twenty canoes, were bent on avenging one of their interpreters who had died unnaturally there.

The province of Senegambia ended with the American War of Independence. Siding with the Thirteen States, the French recaptured Gorée and St Louis, retaking and razing the fort once again in 1779. Senegal's return to France by the Treaty of Versailles in 1783, sporadic raids by French privateers, a brief reoccupation by a sergeant's guard after Waterloo, then in 1829 James Island's final abandonment.

The French in 1779 had, with the bastions, blown up the piles which kept the then three-acre island from erosion. Not only its political rôle has disappeared: its physical area continues to decline. For some time yet, though, this will not prevent one's taking the outboard to the pontoon and wandering up to the roofless walls. The many generations and calibres of cannon – '1753 24 pr', 'Anno 1777', some repositioned, one off shore underwater – are tokens of the fort's vicissitudes. Its patched and hotch-potch architecture – crude mortared masonry, courses of red brick, some windows' lintels and smooth plaster still intact – results from its repeated reconstruction.

Their roots undermining the twenty-foot walls, their bare boughs reaching up to the eleven slits for roof-beams, the baobabs tower as vertical counterparts to the recumbent cannons.

Albreda *alias* Albadarr (from the Arabic for the full moon?) was the island garrison's on-shore antagonist during the Franco-British altercations described above. From the first mud hut permitted by the ruler of Niumi's lease of 1681 (and destroyed by fire in 1686) grew a French trading station that was 'destroyed, rebuilt, burned, rebuilt, overrun and rebuilt again'. At one time the French presence consisted solely of 'two black butlers . . . to hoist their colours every Sunday'; another, of 'only one Frenchwoman, all the men except her husband being dead' (and she having survived five spouses in three years). Until its resident slavers were ruined by the Act of 1807, Albreda (*pace* Alex Haley) must have been a busy entrepôt.

The atmosphere nowadays is more one-hut reminiscent. The CFAO's two-floored 'factory' poses in its frame of baobabs: relinquished to the government for one symbolic dalasi, it still awaits reworking as a museum. By the uprooted tree trunks the locals sun-dry fish, and one of the shacks still bears the shop-sign *'Le Commerce Africain'*. Here stood the flagstaff that, according to the guides, guaranteed the freedom of any slave that touched it. (A Carron eighteen-pounder, inscribed *GR* and made in 1810, recently replaced it.) Here wait the children, held back by the bobby, whose sticky hands pull *Roots* pilgrims on to Juffure

Albreda

Juffure – American *Roots* pilgrims, griot Fofana's widow and Alex Haley's photo

Juffure, to visitors, is a two-faced place. A fascinating object of fact and fiction, it offers, like a play on a revolving stage, two totally different scenarios. Programmed by *Roots*, most pilgrim-spectators enjoy the evocative if primitive Mandinka-village idyll. They dutifully suspend disbelief and wonder at the sight of 'Kunta's bantaba tree', the 'Kinteh Kunda compound' and the widow of griot Fofana who, perched on the ancestral canopied bed and clutching her framed and faded cover-feature magazine, poses as a flesh-and-blood link with our misplaced hero.

But Alex Haley devotees will search in vain for any nearby 'village bolong . . . which took' the Kinte womenfolk 'around a turn into a wider tributary . . . twisting inland from the Gambia River'. They must also turn a blind eye to the 'Portu-guese chapel' and, similarly a stone's throw away, the ancient trading station of Albreda. These are part of Juffure's other décor, that of historical reality. Three hundred years before Kunta Kinte's time the Portuguese established the first Juffure, north-east of the present site and named San Domingo. This in local parlance soon became *San Dimonko*, further corrupted into *Sandi Munko Joyo* as the later local alias for James Island. The two-floored 'Portuguese chapel' was probably a shop, store or home. Visible from the track a half-kilometre on from the Albreda-Juffure crossing, it is one of The Gambia's better ruins: small (ten paces square) but unex-pectedly tall, with neat courses of mortar between its laterite blocks, patches of plaster still intact, a yellow-brick arch over one lower window, and the four above

rectangular beneath their wooden lintel.

The Juffure ceded to the Cour-landers was probably closer to the present-day site. The Dutchmen captured whilst trying to evict them in 1660; Major Holme's soldiers disembarking one year later; the African Company's agents that acquired a plot at 'Gilliflee'; the British garrison of the fort erected here in 1721; the French and English 'factors' who, well into Kunta Kinte's time, 'traded side by side in the village' of 'Gillefree', 'Jithrey' or 'Jillifrey' . . . none lend credibility to the Haley theory that Juffure – 'four days up-river from the coast' – is the authentic birthplace of his historical Gambian ancestor.

Abuko and the Kombos.

The Bakau-Fajara promontory constitutes most of Kombo St Mary, the colonists' 'British Kombo' and the locals' *tubab banko*, with nearby Bathurst as its chief town. The 19th-century 'Upper' or 'Foreign Kombo' consisted of the four districts to the south, which were converted to Islam and first united (by Fodi/Kombo Silla) during the Soninki-Marabout Wars. Called Kombo Dambele Yaa, Kombo Santo, Kombo Afeet and Kombo Naarang, they have since become the North, South, East and Central districts that stretch east to Foni and south to the Casamance.

Bounded to the west by the miles of splendid beach, the Kombos give the capital a pleasant rural hinterland, easily accessible and scenically attractive. Even the name, though typically ambiguous, adds to the milk-and-honey image: *Kom bo* ('the hatred is lifted') or, also in Mandinka, 'dew' viz. 'a land so safe that not even dew will fall on you'. Though temporarily contradicted by the marabouts' warring on both Britain and the Kombos' Soninkis, the two terms indicate how the first Mandinkas found a safe and peaceful haven here after their 14-15th-century trek west.

Cape Point, the Department of Agriculture

Cape Point received its Portuguese alias *Cabo de Santa Maria* from its 15th-century 'discoverers', and the name of St Mary's overflowed to the nearby island when Britain decided on Bathurst. Captain Grant bought a first site on this breezy Cape St Mary to build a convalescent home for the colony's fever-ridden garrison. And to hang a lantern on a lofty palm as the first of the Gambia's navigational aids.

Bakau beach

Bakau is the Mandinkas' *Ba kankungo* (Shore or Coast). It is also a long drawn-out cliff-top township which, with hotels and villas, overlooks beaches and bays.

The Katchikali 'sacred crocodile pool' was revealed to the Mandinka Bojang family by a ruler's sister called Katchikali. She first tested the worthiness of one Nkooping and his sons Jaali and Tambasi by begging them to help retrieve her child, supposedly lost down a well. For showing willing, they were rewarded with the well itself, where 'any woman washed will, providing she sleeps with no other ... before the same time next year bear a child'. Jaali and Tambasi in return rewarded Katchikali with the first thing they caught in their nets: two crocodiles, which their mother put in the well. Seven generations of Bojangs ago, these reptiles (and the water lettuce which soon overgrew the site) were the prelude to the present-day scene. When the water is too little for the crocodiles to submerge, the women to bathe ritually or the Bojangs to make *naso*-potions, there is no lack of helpers to dig deeper. The first were from Madibakunda, 'Bamboo' Madiba's place; for the re-excavation of 1981 volunteers came from all around, an impressive collective effort. In 1985, a bull-dozer was borrowed.

Abuko is synonymous here with wildlife conservation and means, for visitors, the Nature Reserve beside the Lamin Stream. In 1916 its source was fenced to form the Abuko Water Catchment Area; the density of its riverine forest increased in consequence and this attracted game. The attention of the locals, too, who holed the fence and poked in their pigs to feed, illegally tapped the protected palms for toddy and, worse, took to poaching. When in 1967 a leopard made these mis-demeanours dangerous, one wily Kalilu called on the wildlife conservation officer to shoot it for 'killing domestic pigs'. The latter, Eddie Brewer, was led through a hole in the fence to the scene of the crime, accompanied by his daughter Stella who continues the story: 'I compare that hole ... with Alice's Looking-Glass, for beyond we discovered an incredible world we had not known existed. With each step we became more enchanted by what we saw. We were walking from the familiar savannah into the cool, damp

Long-crested hawk eagle

Cattle egrets in nuptial plumage

The Bambo Pool, Abuko

Abuko

Saturnis moth

Abyssinian roller

Purple-headed glossy starling

help of the telescope in the upstairs gallery, Nile crocodiles and monitors can easily be seen, a fair number of Abuko's 277 bird species or even the Western sitatunga, five of which have been 'imported' (and one of which features in the Wildlife Department's crest).

Tight, eerie jungle follows. Off left (reassurance for the claustrophobic) there are at first snatches of the open bright savanna, but soon one is engulfed by a wondrous lush dark world. Stepping over massive roots, edging round mighty trunks, one hears or glimpses the many monkeys; some, like the squirrels, may scamper over the path, snakes rustle safely away, butterflies and birds flutter in brilliant contrast to the chiaroscuro.

Busumbala. Derivations and associations are, again, of more substance than the present-day place: *Busi mba* ('taken by force from my mother') because the first 'king' here kidnapped a neighbouring chieftain's daughter in order to help him increase the population of his new-found town. Busumbala was the scene of several Soninki-Marabout skirmishes (Archer writing that its subjects in May 1855 attacked and killed the king of Kombo, Gray maintaining it was marabouts from Gunjur who attacked Busumbala, and not in May but June). Again in 1894 the place required forcible pacification.

Brikama in Bainunka means Women's Town, the governmental quarter established here for the matriarchal locals' former female rulers. Soninki animists, Brikama's Mandinkas stood long and firm against the Muslim marabouts. Their township (officially 'a clean and flourishing place') was stormed for the first (recorded) time and completely demolished by the war-lords of Gunjur in 1854. By 1873 these henchmen of Fodi Kabba's controlled every Foreign Kombo settlement save Brikama and Busumbala. Tomani Bojang, ruler of the former, even offered *in extremis* to cede his lands in return for British protection, but this – with his troops embarked in 1870 and only a 100-man constabulary left – Administrator Callaghan was unable to provide. In mid-1874 Brikama fell, in June 1875

atmosphere of a tropical rain forest'. Their immediate desire to preserve this 'glimpse of what The Gambia must once have looked like' was realized in March 1968 when a 'receptive and sympathetic government' agreed to establish the reserve. Its area was extended from 180 to 252 acres in 1978 and enclosed in an eight-foot wire fence with the help of the World Wildlife Fund.

In the first loose forest of the drier savanna, trunks are caked with mud by the tree-ants and treetops decked with their 'nests'. The path soon drops to the main Bambo Pool, pretty with White water-lilies and statuesque with palms. Planks take one across a swampy side-stream and steps up to the first photo hide and the education centre, a cool green 'colonial' structure, fronted by a defunct fountain and planned in 1970 as the reserve's rest house. With the

Sun-drying fresh fish at Gunjur

Busumbala also. Chief Bojang and his Soninki subjects sought refuge in British Kombo. Though disarmed, they built a stockade at Lamin, whereupon Fodi Silla sent a threat to 'pursue them to Cape St Mary and destroy them'. The rains saved the colony: they broke and so stopped play. As a diplomatic alternative to certain military defeat, Sir Samuel Rowe presented Tomani with an ultimatum: on 29 September 1875, rather than evacuate the Kombos, he 'agreed to shave his head, become a marabout, adopt a Muslim name, lay down his arms and destroy his stockade'. With Fodi Silla thus assuaged and the British colony reprieved, the Kombos' two centuries of unbroken Bojang rule came to an end. Fodi Silla's counter-undertaking to let the Soninkis cultivate in peace (and his good-behaviour bonus of £50 per annum) was forgotten by the 1890s, when he 'reverted to his old ways' of robbery with violence and internecine tribal fighting. Now however the stronger protectorate was able to take the retaliatory action that led to Fodi Silla's capture, exile and death, and to the reinstatement of a local Bojang chief.

Gunjur is a pleasant and spacious place, a relative metropolis with its 'high street' and petrol station, two roadside mosques and two roadside markets. To clear the site, the locals say, the first settlers had to raze a termite-mound, *tungo/guru* viz. 'anthill/demolish' becoming the *Tunjuru* from which *Gunjur* derives.

In the second half of the 19th century Gunjur was a marabout base and thus, for British officialdom, a 'hotbed of insurrection'. Fodi Kabba originated here, starting his long inglorious career a lieutenant in Maba's army, and being first mentioned in (British) dispatches by Governor O'Connor in 1855. Fodi Silla was finally routed here, too, in the expeditionary force's successful second attack. If all this is ephemeral and past, marabout religiosity survives in the nearby 'holy places', which for visitors form the principal interest of this chief town of Kombo South.

Newly-painted 'Gambi-boats' at Tanji

83

Kenye-Kenye Jamango ('Mosque soil') was made holy by the sojourn of one Shaikh Omar Futiu in the late 1830s. It overlooks a magnificent sweep of beach, with (relative) home comforts for the many pilgrims who spend up to a year here: praying in the palm-frond mosque, sleeping in the breeze-block shack, drawing fresh water from cement-rimmed wells and relaxing at the ritual bantaba.

Tanji one often perceives from afar, thanks to the smoke (and smell) produced by its 'fish curing site'. The photogenic beach is liveliest late afternoon when the fishing-crews come home. Children play, girls gut fish and, beneath the twisted baobabs, the Serers repair their long bright boats and stretch their nets on wooden frames to dry. The self-styled 'sipriters' (shipwrights!) nail the long mahogany planks and caulk them with *tuppa*, a rope-and-cotton 'filler'. The sides are painted gay with names, dates and/or Arabic imprecations, a crescent moon (the Cross of Islam) or a random geometry of triangles and squares with a face just discernible somewhere.

The fish-curing sheds behind are neither sightly nor fragrant. If not averse to smoke or kipper-smells, one can enter and see the procedure . . . once the eyes have grown accustomed to the gloom. Piles of fire-wood stand outside: the wooden sheds sometimes make it redundant by catching fire themselves.

Kartung's claim to sacrosanctity is the Folonko crocodile pool. It 'functions' like Katchikali's, is similarly covered with *pakanju* water lettuce and has resident reptiles equally unpredictable. But its site is fractionally more dramatic and, being remoter, less encumbered with suburban youths and trash. The authorities have enclosed Folonko's enclave with a high wire fence, and in 1980 half encircled the pool itself with a breeze-block wall. Steps down enable 'people to perform the ritual bath, wash their hair and drink a bit of the water. These people are mainly barren women or people with stomach trouble'. On the camp-fire crescent of cement blocks and logs, shady beneath the *kobo*-figs and palms, one can sit and wait for a sight of the white crocodile.

Fish curing (viz. kippering) at Tanji

The Atlantic coast south of Tanji

Nile crocodile

Sun-dried fish pell-mell at Ghana Town

Ghana Town is self-explanatory, but a grandiose name for a fairly minor place. The hamlet, inland, is little more than a malodorous acre in which sundry fish dry on palm-frond platforms and, dried, are then stacked flat. On the beach, however, is the unexpected sight of thousand upon thousand of superb orange-pink shells smashed and dumped. The living molluscs are fetched in here by the boat-load, brought ashore in buckets on the women's heads, piled on the sand and there sorted, shelled and sold. Given what visitors pay for these *cymbium glans,* the locals must be discarding a small fortune.

Sanneh-Mentering is another sacred place a short walk from Ghana Town. Preferably accompanied by the alkalu of Brufut, one reaches the cliff-top clearing with its massive baobab. Graffiti are carved in the trunk, by Allied soldiers who were warned of Sanneh's sanctity and 'punished for their impiety'. While those who left their initials 'suffered indescribably all night' (from mosquitoes?) the patriot who put 'Scotland for Ever' was killed soon thereafter, self-righteous locals say (a fairly safe bet for divine retribution in time of war).

The stone at the foot of the baobab is for alms: a few bututs from tourists, kola-nuts, cloth or a slave from the pilgrims who come in the hope of a baby or more profitable business. A fertility-bringing wash costs three dalasis, a week-long vigil in the mud hut, in abstinence until the alkalu returns with a sacrificial sheep: 75.

I had the luck to arrive once at the same time as a group of young wives from Gunjur. Beautifully dressed, all gold on silk and satin, they came with a biddy carrying her knick-knacks in a halved gourd. They first prayed and placed their coins beside the baobab, then filed down steeply for the ritual washing in sea-water – a solemn, impressive procession between the lofty lines of palms.

Off-loading the fishing-boats, Ghana Town (right)

Sanneh-Mentering, descending for a fertility-bringing bathe (opposite)

Bintang one reaches by an excellent laterite track marked, 50 kilometres from Banjul, on the south-bank road to Basse. Of the base built here by Cromwell's patentees in the 1650s; the 'Vintan/Vintang' of the Portuguese mulattos; the factory permitted to the French by the Jola king of Foni in 1717 (and retaken by Britain in 1724), of Mungo Park's 'Vintain' of 1795, the present-day inhabitants know nothing. In the absence of local guides, one looks for historical spoor: a site near the bolong, any trading station's life-line; ideally on an eminence, for cool-ness and ease of defence; perhaps surrounded by baobabs (from seeds placed in Portuguese tombs) . . . and sure enough, left of the jetty, the small hill is strewn with masonry: ancient slabs still faced with plaster and a monolithic six-foot length of runnel. Atop the hill the four rings of stones mark modern graves.

Bwiam is named after its original owner, one Bwiamu Sambu. Apart from the stores' cooled Vimto and Anti Worm Elixir, the Jola hamlet's only interest is its enigmatic iron pot. Found (with local help) beside the track precisely two kilometres from the mosque, the pot protrudes like the conning-tower of a buried submarine. Some *tubab* (foreigners), the locals tell you, once dug all day without working it free. 'And when they returned to dig next day, the soil was back in place around the pot.' Three stumps (inverted legs?) rise from its bird-limed top; in time of war the rusting pot turns so that its aperture indicates the quarter of the enemy's attack. 'Even us youngsters, if we want a special favour, definitely come here and make a special prayer and donate 50 bututs or maybe a chewing-stick.'

Tankular. Under the baobabs, the men make bricks and hack dug-outs with their hoes; on the muddy beach new boats 'soak', filled with water. Shrimp-traps are slung to dry in the stunted mango and in the lowly waterfront compound (where women sit smoking pipes with babies on their backs) hangs the hamlet's only curiosity: a nondescript ship's bell, dating from 1711 and endowed with the power of ringing itself whenever an enemy or shipwreck threatens. A scrap of compensation for the track from Sankandi is the better-founded information that near by stood a Portuguese trading station.

Toniataba is reached by a winding track that, marked off the Basse road 150 kilometres from Banjul, enters 'town' via the locked and mud-walled tombs of Wuli Fatty's family. Those desirous of praying for favours on their graves will have to fetch the key from Hajji Fudali Fatty. This fine octogenarian, white-robed and fingering his 'rosary' of beads, is usually found in the remarkable round house. He is the last son of Shaikh Othman, a famous Mandinka marabout and alleged purveyor of jujus to Fodi Kabba and Musa Mollo. They would visit him, so the story goes, in this very house: a vast cone of thatch on six-foot walls 60 paces in circumference, supported inside by split bamboos, cement-floored and divided by once-white-washed mud partitions. Frequently rebuilt, it is the subject of appeals on Radio Gambia whenever volunteers are needed for repairs.

With an interpreter, and shoes removed, one is welcomed in to hear its history: 'When Shaikh Othman *alias* Jimbiti Fatty *alias* Wuli Musa Fatty died, his son Lamin Fatty moved in. He died 120 years old and the next son, Kemu Fatty, inherited. He died at 130 and the house passed to Hajji Fudali' . . . I trusted he would live to at least 140 and was reminded of Dr Galloway's remark that 'Chronology is perhaps the weakest aspect of oral history, which tends to "telescope" lists, while genealogy tends to "expand" it again'. The place-name should at least bear out the Hajji: *Tonia*, Mandinka for Truth, which one pledged oneself to tell beneath its *taba* (kola-tree).

Written history is no more satisfactory, for Archer narrates anachronistically (and Gray ignores entirely) an engagement recorded in Banjul's old government cemetery: here lies 'Captain Alexander Sankey Roberts of the 1st Battalion West India Regt. who . . . was mortally wounded at the capture of Tonia-taba . . . on 28th April 1892'.

Kataba Fort survives as a reminder of Britain's colonial confrontations in both Salum and Badibu. After king Kolli had ceded MacCarthy Island, his hostile neighbour Kementeng/Kemintang proved increasingly troublesome. His technique of settling commercial disputes by seizing the merchants' schooners led in 1834 to the Governor's banning trade above MacCarthy Island. Kementeng even acquired two cannons abandoned by the MacCarthy Island Militia and the men of HMS *Brisk* who in June of that year failed to locate him and retreated, not defeated but in disarray. In April 1841, Governor Huntley's expedition was rather more auspicious: faced with a joint attack by Kementeng, the Fulas and Bambara raiders, the king of Kataba welcomed the British force, signed a treaty of friendship and commerce and gave land for the building of the fort. Its garrison from the 3rd West Indian Regiment so effectively imposed peace as to be no longer needed twelve months later.

The south-bank ferry to MacCarthy Island and Georgetown

Georgetown was built, a mud-brick township, when king Kolli in 1823 ceded to Britain the island of Janjangbure ('Refuge'). First christened Lemain(e), it was later renamed in honour of Sir Charles MacCarthy, the African administrator so opposed to slavery that, by pressurizing a reluctant Earl of Bathurst, he succeeded in having Grant sent from Gorée and Bathurst built. Whether Georgetown commemorates Britain's third Hanoverian, who had recently died after ten years of madness, or his heir George IV, 'an undutiful son, bad husband and callous father, least regretted by those who knew him best', really does not matter.

As the headquarters of MacCarthy Island Division, The Gambia's unofficial 'up-country capital' still has much of an old-time trading outpost. The post office might have been an English chapel with its doorway Gothic-arched. Beside it, the old government rest house has the customary corrugated iron distinguished by unusual whirls and frills. The Home Government of the 1820s may have boggled at permanent building, resting content with the island's mud-brick Fort George and Fort Fatota, but the DC's headquarters is a splendid colonial pile.

The desultory main street runs parallel to the river: from the post office and police post one can walk upstream between the terraces of tailors, an open-air museum of vintage sewing-machines. With Emett-like relics of disused mill machinery incongruous on its playground, the long and yellow buildings of the Methodist Church and primary school seem a disappointing upshot to the years and endeavours that the Wesleyans spent here. Permitted by the king of Kataba to quarry mainland rock after 1827, merchants from Bathurst built the first stores and John Morgan the first mission station. Its congregation was swelled by the Liberated Africans and discharged soldiers settled up river. Its educational mission grew into the famous Chiefs' School reserved for the *seyfolu*'s sons (and rebuilt by the government in 1927). Then renamed the Armitage High School, it remains The Gambia's only secondary boarding establishment.

The roofless hulk of the so-called 'slave market' is conspicuous on the north bank. Not only self-appointed guides, even knowledgeable elders point out the wall-rings for 'the shackled and manacled slaves' inside. They are more likely to have served, I think, for bolting the doors or hitching horses. Apart from East Africa's crudely walled pens, physical vestiges of the slave-trade are few. The reason is simple: as a non-perishable commodity, human beings did not need expensive entrepôts. Gables here indicate a once-ridged roof, to keep rain off precious trading goods, not slaves; a slave-pen would not have been, as this is, floored with tiles; the regular arched doorways, neatly rimmed in brick, and generous windows subsequently blocked are scarcely compatible with a prison.

Only those who brave the Georgetown ferry and the track through Karantaba have a chance of making out the plaque on the Mungo Park Memorial: 'Near this spot Mungo Park set out on the 2nd December 1795 and the 4th May 1805 on his travels to explore the course of the Niger'. The spot was Pisania, a then-prosperous, long-vanished trading station. In December 1795, after six months of acclimatizing, convalescing and learning Mandinka at the home of one Dr Laidley, the 24-year-old Scottish doctor commenced the lonely and epic trek recounted modestly yet with polished detail by his *Travels in the Interior Districts of Africa*. The second departure in 1805 was again under the auspices of the African Association, but this *Mission to the Interior of Africa* had military and political objectives also. Park was given a commission and an escort of 250 soldiers 'for the purpose of dislodging the French from Albreda . . . of re-establishing English factories in the River Gambia, and of extending the relations of commerce with that and the neighbouring countries'. Frequently at loggerheads with the African Corps' Lieutenant Martyn and encumbered by his retinue (a clumsy contrast to the first journey's black boy, two donkeys and one horse), Park reached the Niger with only Martyn and three half-crazed soldiers still alive. His journal stops short on 16 November 1805 when, near Bussa, all were waylaid and killed.

Basse, the riverside market and disused trading station

Basse. The well-built quarters of the former trading companies stand imposing but abandoned on the bank. From the lofty trees beside them, kapok is collected in February and March: lorries loaded with the white floss you see ferried from the north bank by the blue and white *Johe,* the wooden 50-footer built in 1961. Beside the usual rhun-palm jetty, passengers are paddled across in the type of steel dinghy the Allies used over the Rhine.

For the Thursday-morning market the bank is covered in earthenware: delivered by donkey-cart from Alohungari and carried away on the heads of the girls that buy them, platters, bowls, cullenders and African amphorae make a photogenic display. The court house alongside, corrugated iron on columns, becomes an *ad hoc* emporium of roasted groundnuts and pumpkins as plump as the pots. Reeds and bamboo lie behind the 'square', due to be made into krinting.

Down stream, tugs wait for their dozen lighters to be filled with groundnuts from the GPMB depot. Its eight bins, each for 700 tons, were built in 1974 when the GPMB took over here from the private buyers (and turned its hand also to cotton). Brought in by road from group farmers and co-operatives, screened, twice weighed and 'quality controlled', the nuts finally reach the rubber 'evacuation belt' that may chute up to 200 tons at a time into the sturdier lighters.

All this is Basse Duma Su, *Basse/ Bassa* being a mat (on which the town's founder, one General Tiramakang, reportedly first rested). *Duma Su* (Lower Home) is literally this quarter that ventured down to the riverside in the dry season. The rains used to flood it and then Basse shrank to *Santu Su* (Upper Home). The town's better half, it lies a short walk inland.

The Gambia ferry at Basse

Fatoto. After 1934 the mail brought up by the Travelling Post Office aboard the weekly steamer was carried on from Basse by a 'travelling postman' who, if he cycled fast enough, reached Fatoto twelve hours later. Modern visitors to Basse need only an hour or two's sortie for this 'roadhead' in The Gambia's eastern reaches. A Mandinka-Fula-Serahuli village, Fatoto in Mandinka means 'spread out', which it is, between the mast-topped hill and the baobabs along the swamp. The market has signs of life; on the dramatic banks where the deep-cleft track ends, women wash, cattle wallow and a tiny ferry shuttles when it must. But in between there is little but dereliction. The premises of this once-flourishing trading station stand starkly photogenic but sad. Three colonnaded beside the track, three detached on the cliff top, they were impressively built. But their walls of brick or mortared stone, still in places plastered, are now ugly with graffiti; their crumbling tiled or red-brick floors are littered; concrete lintels top doorways and windows long removed, and scales made by *'B. Trayvou . . . Lyon'* rust in warehouses wide open to the sky. With the air of a Western ghost-town, this easternmost administrative centre has now more cows than humans.

Fatoto (above)

Basse, groundnut tug and lighter loading (right)

Home by boat with pots bought at Basse market

The Stone Circles are a

Senegambian enigma. Though similar, isolated structures are found in the Sahara and as far south as Guinea, the largest known concentration lies scattered north of the Gambia in its mid-river region: clusters of laterite columns, numbering from ten to 24 and many still standing up to nine feet high. Despite their abundance, the lack of inscriptions and associated objects has frustrated several semi-specialist expeditions.

Speculation as to their age ('pre-Islamic viz. 15th-century but post-neolithic'/'as old as 100 years BC') was cut short by recent carbon-14 tests which dated the circles to approximately AD 750. Skeletons found in the central graves make them unquestionably burial sites. But these, the only facts we have, themselves pose further problems. The graves are older than the circles; the average height of their negroid incumbents (an impressive 5' 9")

suggests a Bantu origin from the south, while all analogous megalithic cultures are found to the north: in Mesopotamia 3000 years BC, in the Egypt of the pyramids, at Stonehenge and Avesbury, on Malta and even the Canary Islands as late as the 14th century.

Few accept that a tall black race originated here, evolved the Circles without outside influence and developed the iron implements buried in the graves and used to shape the stones. The region, apart from a few modern mosques, has no other monuments. What lofty southern immigrants buried their dead here with copper and iron artifacts (the trappings of kingship) and evidence of human sacrifice; later returned to mark the sites with designs derived north of the Sahara and, leaving no clue as to the significance, moved on?

Oral history viz. local tradition has it that the builders were of Egyptian origin. Travelling with an intelligent

driver taught me that the comments of visiting specialists soon become local lore; one Captain Duchemin engaged Gambians in a two-month study in 1906; several French and British teams have since explored the area with Gambian diggers and guides, and conversational speculation might well be already part of the gospel according to the griots. (Their 'curse' on those who disturb these tombs of the 'ancient gods/giants' was vindicated, or inspired, by the prompt death of a certain Captain Doke and two other excavators.)

Apart from the carbon-14 dating and the physical finds, expedition reports contain little more than intelligent topographical guesswork: that relatively few workers could have quickly chiselled even the largest ten-ton columns because freshly quarried laterite is soft (hardening only after exposure to the air); that taller stones were slid into upright position by means of an

encircling trench (because the same
stones have fallen back outwards into
the trenches' soft refill). What is more
challenging and as yet unknown is
why designs and sizes vary, with
stones from two to nine feet high and
from one to four feet in diameter,
with circles of ten to 24 stones
measuring twelve-twenty feet across;
why Ker Bach has a monolithic
V-shape, why others are topped by a
cup-shaped depression, this fitted in
some cases with a neat stone ball.

Stone Circles, at Lamin Koto (left)
and Wassu

Index